IMPRINTING

OUR

IMAGE

IMPRINTING
OUR
IMAGE

AN INTERNATIONAL ANTHOLOGY
BY WOMEN WITH DISABILITIES

edited by

DIANE DRIEDGER and SUSAN GRAY

gynergy books

ISBN 0-921881-22-3

This book was printed
on recycled paper containing
deinked fibres.

COVER GRAPHIC ILLUSTRATION:
Catherine O'Neill of Emerging Design, Ottawa
EDITOR:
Lynn Henry
DESIGN:
Catherine Matthews
PRINTER:
Best Gagné Book Manufacturers Inc.

Second printing 1997

Printed and bound in Canada.

With thanks to the Canada Council for its kind support.

CANADIAN CATALOGUING IN PUBLICATION DATA
Main entry under title:

Imprinting our image
ISBN 0-921881-22-3

1. Handicapped women. I. Driedger, Diane Lynn, 1960-
II. Gray, Susan, 1960-

HV1569.3.W65I67 1992   362.4'082   C92-098670-6

CREDITS

The following articles were originally published elsewhere:

Theresia Degener: "Sterile Without Consent," first appeared in *Connexions*, (Winter 1987), and appears here with permission.

Susan Gray Dueck, "On Life with an Invisible Disability," first appeared in *Breaking the Silence*, April D'Aubin, ed. Winnipeg: COPOH, 1988, and appears here with permission.

Lesley Hall, "Beauty Quests—A Double Disservice: Beguiled, Beseeched and Bombarded, Challenging the Concept of Beauty," first appeared in *Women and Disability: An Issue*, Women with Disabilities Feminist Collective, eds. Melbourne: Women with Disabilities Feminist Collective, 1987. It appears here with permission.

Mikiko Misono, "My Life Story," first appeared in *Report of DPI Asia/Pacific Leadership Training Seminar, Oct. 11-15, 1986*, Disabled Peoples' International Asia/Pacific Regional Council, ed. Tokyo: DPI Asia/Pacific Regional Council, 1986. It appears here with permission.

Judith Snow: "Living At Home," first appeared in *Canadian Journal on Mental Retardation 35* (Autumn 1985), and appears here with permission. This journal is now called *entourage* and its address is: The G. Allan Roeher Institute, York University, Kinsmen Bldg., 4700 Keele Street, Downsview, Ontario, M3J IP3.

Amber Coverdale Sumrall: "Crossing the High Country," first appeared in *Kaleidescope 16* (Spring 1988).

Jayne Whyte: "Pictures of Women and Mental Health," first appeared in *Breaking the Silence*, April D'Aubin, ed. Winnipeg: COPOH, 1988, and appears here with permission.

ACKNOWLEDGEMENTS

WE ARE GRATEFUL TO the women with disabilities who contributed to this anthology. Without you, there would be no book. We also appreciate the financial support of the Disabled People's Concerns Desk of the Mennonite Central Committee and the moral support of its former director, Henry Enns. The support of the Coalition of Provincial Organizations of the Handicapped (COPOH) of Canada, in loans of computer equipment and staff co-operation, was vital to the completion of this book. Thanks are also due to April D'Aubin of COPOH for her support.

Finally, we thank the international advisory committee of women with disabilities who reviewed and commented on the manuscript—Dr. Fatima Shah (Pakistan), Eileen Giron (El Salvador) and Ann-Marit Saeboenes (Norway).

CONTENTS

INTRODUCTION

Having a disability is no more of a tragedy than having green eyes. What is a tragedy is the lack of sensitivity, awareness and knowledge that disabled women encounter, and the physical, psychological and social barriers that result.

— Pat Danforth *Canada*
   (From "Women with Disabilities," in *The Healthsharing Book: Resources for Canadian Women*, Kathleen McDonnell and Mariana Valverde, eds. Toronto: Women's Press, 1985, pp. 180-81.)

WOMEN WITH DISABILITIES EXPERIENCE two oppressions: they are women and they are disabled. They have been silenced on both fronts. *Imprinting Our Image* is a collection of writings by women with disabilities who are renaming the world according to their own experiences.

Women from many regions of the world have contributed writing and artwork to this book. Some have chosen to describe ways in which they have coped with their environment. Others describe the inroads they have made in their own development or changes they have helped create in the attitudes and policies of their societies.

The women differ widely in cultural perspectives and this has been, for us as the editors, one of the most interesting and challenging aspects of this project. *Imprinting Our Image* was begun in 1986 when we realized the necessity for a book written by disabled women from a variety of cultures. We began with a strong conviction about the importance of disabled women telling their stories to the world, a belief in the inherent significance of each woman's story, and a conviction about the power of writing.

It was a tremendous challenge for us to ensure that the manuscripts submitted by women of widely varying backgrounds were handled in ways that would bring out their strengths and reflect their unique cultural viewpoints and writing styles. We learned a great deal in the process of revising submissions so that they could be as clear as possible while retaining the beauty of the original manuscripts. For instance, a woman in China, we quickly found, does not phrase things in the same way as a woman from Canada.

All the women submitted manuscripts written in English—we were careful to specify this as a requirement at the time of solicitation since we lacked the resources to translate submissions. Some of the women were able to write in English; others arranged for translations in their own countries. In a few instances, interviews with women with disabilities were carried out by non-disabled women, and in several countries some women with disabilities formed self-help groups in the course of writing their submissions. In some cases, lack of money and equipment made writing conditions difficult, but in spite of this the women submitted and re-submitted the manuscripts that now comprise this book.

It is important to note that the world, its political borders, laws, and even the lives of the writers have changed, and continue to change since some of these manuscripts were submitted. For example, at the time the two women from Germany wrote, their country was not unified, hence their references to West Germany.

Finally, to ensure a balance of perspectives between the developing and developed parts of the world, the manuscript was examined by an advisory committee consisting of women with disabilities from a variety of countries and backgrounds: Eileen Giron (El Salvador); Ann-Marit Saeboenes (Norway); and Dr. Fatima Shah (Pakistan).

Imprinting Our Image is organized around the central theme that women with disabilities are citizens with rich perspectives and talents, and the means to contribute to their societies. Rather than living in a world that, too often, looks right through them, disabled women are becoming a force in their own right. It is our hope that this book will spur them to emerge as did Athena—fully clothed and uttering a loud cry. In its organization, the book deals with the process of such empowerment.

We have organized the book into five sections. The first section, "Our Image in the Family," examines the constraints and barriers placed within the family on women with disabilities—constraints both parental and marital. Section two, "Our Image in the Community," expands from family barriers to the image of women with disabilities in the community, and shows how women have coped with these barriers. Section three, "Imprinting Our Image on the World," discusses how women with disabilities have made their imprint through careers, art and writing. Section four, "In Spite of the World," exposes societal expectations that women must fulfill the "body beautiful" image to be acceptable, sexual and powerful.

Finally, the last section of the book, "Dealing with the World," reflects upon the growing worldwide disabled peoples' movement for change. Since the mid-1970s, people with various disabilities have organized in over one hundred countries to speak out about their own concerns. Disabled Peoples' International (DPI) is the manifestation of this global movement. And women with disabilities have played an important part in this development, by forming groups and spearheading initiatives to have their voices heard both as disabled people and as women. In addition, in 1990 a new World Coalition of Women with Disabilities emerged at the first United Nations Seminar on Women with Disabilities in Vienna. There, women formed their own organization to represent the unique concerns of women with disabilities.

For too long academics and writers have written "about" women with disabilities without consulting the women themselves. For too long medical professionals and social workers have done *to* disabled people or written *about* them. This is doubly true of disabled women—as women, they have been more silent, as society teaches women to be. Until just a few years ago, very few women with disabilities were writing about themselves, their histories and experience, and their philosophies of liberation. Slowly this situation is beginning to change.

This introduction would not be complete if we did not address the question of who we, the editors, are. Both of us have histories that have involved interest in and commitment to the women's movement and the disability movement.

Diane has been a non-disabled ally in the disabled persons' movement for the last twelve years. A strong proponent of social movements for change, Diane also wrote her Master's thesis in history on Disabled Peoples' International. Entitled *The Last Civil Rights Movement*, it was published in 1989. She worked for seven years with DPI in its founding stages, and subsequently worked in the Development Office, Chairperson's office and the North American and Caribbean Regional Office in Jamaica.

While in Jamaica in 1988, she helped organize the first leadership training seminar for disabled women in the region. During that time, she continued to work on this book. The manuscript and letters from contributors survived Hurricane Gilbert, as did Diane. Upon her return to Winnipeg, Diane began work with the Coalition of Provincial Organizations of the Handicapped (COPOH) as International Development Officer. In her work there, she has helped co-ordinate literacy training for women with disabilities in Central America. Diane has recently joined the board of the Canadian Research Institute for the Advancement of Women (CRIAW). And her most recent brush with a (hopefully) short-term back problem has impressed upon her the limitations imposed by the environment. Her forays into her own poetry have further taught her that holding fast to one's voice is important for self-esteem and identity.

Susan, similarly, has found that her creative writing has strengthened her identity. She has had a bleeding disability since birth. She became acquainted with the disability movement in 1986 when she went to work with the Independent Living Resource Centre (ILRC), a consumer-controlled non-profit group made up of, for, and by people with disabilities. The organization is dedicated to helping disabled people integrate into society. In 1987, she went on to work with another disability organization, where she continued her interests in promoting integration. In 1990, Susan served as a consultant on COPOH's and ACOGIPRI's (El Salvador) Central American Literacy project for women with disabilities. She became convinced that empowerment can be accomplished only through the union and work of people with disabilities.

Susan's heritage is a reflection of mixed cultural background and expression. Her father is a white, English-speaking Protestant Canadian. Her mother is East Indian, brought up in Trinidad. Susan's roots on her mother's side are Hindu and her family experience also reflects a large measure of colonialism, since her grandparents were Christianized by Presbyterian missionaries. This ethnic and cultural mixture, which has generated a lifelong interest in cross-cultural study, helped Susan enormously in the work this book entailed.

On surveying this collection, we are repeatedly struck by the spirit of optimism that pervades the writing and the quest of each woman not only for survival, but for dynamism and enrichment in her life. In these pages, for the first time, women with disabilities from different countries in every region of the world have pooled their experiences, philosophies and unquenchable spirit. In the process, they have imprinted their image on the world.

— Diane Driedger and Susan Gray *Winnipeg, Canada* Fall, 1992

I

OUR IMAGE IN THE FAMILY

So the blind girl leads a vegetable existence with nothing to look forward to, except a dependent life as a burden on the charity of parents or relatives. She is usually hidden from visitors and strangers because the family is ashamed of her ...

— Dr. Fatima Shah *Pakistan*

When men become disabled, the marriage breakup is fifty percent; when women become disabled, the marriage breakup is ninety-nine percent.

— Jill Weiss *Canada*
("Disabled Women," in *Women with Disability, Resources for Feminist Research 14*, March 1983: pp. 1-6).

OUR GENUS, OUR ORIGIN, is the family—we are born into it and socialized in it. In this section, women with disabilities from Pakistan, Japan, Bangladesh, Brazil and Canada explain how the family views disabled girls and women, and how this view limits opportunity.

Dr. Fatima Shah of Pakistan relates that disabled girls are seen as useless burdens, and damaged goods in the marriage market. As well, the disabled girl may limit the marriage opportunities of the whole family. Fatima further explains that disabled girls and women lead cloistered existences, hidden away because of family shame.

Yukiko Oka Nakanishi adds that in Japan girls with disabilities are not expected to marry. She writes about how her parents expected her to take jobs they thought would make her most independent. Women with leprosy from Brazil tell stories of their families' fear of leprosy and denial that it exists, even at the risk of not treating it. They discuss their roles as mothers and wives in their communities and how they have persevered in spite of medical and familial ignorance.

Bonita Janzen Friesen reveals how women with disabilities in Bangladesh experience marriage breakdown and the loss of their children. She shows how one woman, Helen Mendes, has been labelled mentally handicapped.

Finally, Jayne C.M. Whyte of Canada discusses how both she and a friend experienced difficulties in their marriages while living with mental illness. They both restructured familial relationships in the process, and Jayne also formed a new network of people to support her life in the community.

All in all, the women in this section are active, integral parts of their families. Their relationships have strength and dynamism as they imprint their unique personalities on those around them.

THE BLIND WOMAN, HER FAMILY AND PARTICIPATION IN THE COMMUNITY (RURAL)

Dr. Fatima Shah
PAKISTAN

THROUGHOUT THE AGES, in every race, religion and culture, women have played a significant role in the family as daughters, sisters, wives and mothers. In enlightened civilizations they have enjoyed a certain status by virtue of this role. Even in the not-so-enlightened cultures, in spite of their subjugation, women have been in fact if not in word, consciously or unconsciously, the custodians of manners and morals in the family and security within the home.

Whether extolled by poets and writers, lauded by orators and weighed in the balance by sociologists, or ignored by society at large, the role they play is of such importance that the word "family" has become more or less synonymous with the word "woman." In the Eastern rural home the woman's role has been even more significant by virtue of the fact that she is almost invariably bound to and confined within the four walls of her home.

To underline the importance of her role seems merely to state what is glaringly obvious. But what appears to be crystal clear in the world of the sighted may be less distinct in the world of the blind, especially the world of the blind woman.

Let us examine the lot of the blind female with special reference to the role assigned to her, in comparison with her sighted peer within the family in the developing regions. It may be mentioned here that over eighty percent of the population of the developing world lives in rural areas, and a great majority of blind women belong there. Therefore we shall concentrate on their problems and needs.

We find that in almost any present day society, but especially in the rural areas of the East, loss of sight for a female is almost always accompanied by loss of status, privileges and rights both in society and within the family.

In society, discrimination against women in general reaches its peak against blind women in particular. This, coupled with prejudice and ignorance, relegates her to the position of an inferior being, an object of false pity and mindless charity. In the family she is deprived of her normal role because of the belief that her disability renders her incapable of performing it.

This loss of place and privilege may be incurred at any stage from infancy to adulthood, depending on when sight is lost. Accordingly, the influences, attitudes and stereotyped beliefs by which the blind are hemmed in by the sighted, will affect her development and personality in various ways and in varying degrees. The amount of harm resulting from these combined factors are dependent on the stage at which the disability begins.

As an infant she is deprived of any special efforts to help her achieve an intelligent awareness of and adjustment to her surroundings. On her own she learns to relate to life and people, through the sounds and smells of daily life. The deep-rooted belief that she is the product of some sin committed by her parents and that she must, therefore, be endured with resignation and patience, seeps into her subconscious and leaves an inevitable and indelible impact on her being and her self-respect.

As a child in the average rural home or even in the cities of the developing regions of the world, she is just left to exist in a confined area of the house. Her movements are far more restricted than those of the male blind child because of the traditional precepts about girls as a whole. Very few, if any, blind girls have the chance to receive any kind of education. Some may be given religious instruction of a limited kind. However, this is more to inculcate in them resignation to their fate rather than to accomplish anything else. Their talents and abilities, instead of being developed and cultivated, remain unexplored, unsounded and perhaps even undetected, if not deliberately suppressed or ignored.

So the blind girl leads a vegetable existence with nothing to look forward to, except a dependent life as a burden on the charity of parents or relatives. She is usually hidden from visitors and strangers because the family is ashamed of her and because, if the fact that there is a blind girl in the family were to become known, it might prove to be an obstacle in arranging the marriages of her siblings and a hindrance to them in their lives. As she approaches maturity and adulthood, the prospect is even bleaker. The cultural patterns and traditions in the developing regions and rural areas are such that it is only after marriage that a woman gains the freedom to play an active role in the community and to be "socially integrated" as it is understood in the West. Social and cultural traditions also dictate that marriages be arranged. This is especially true of the rural areas. Attitudes are so warped and ignorance so rampant that few people would dream of marrying off a blind daughter or of seeking a blind girl as a daughter-in-law. In this way, the blind woman in this part of the world is deprived even of her traditional role of wife and mother, which is surely the birthright of every daughter of Eve.

This deprivation has, naturally, unfortunate psychological repercussions and inflicts on her the added burden of frustration, self-pity and inhibition. The victim of hypercustodialism, always conscious of her lack of a place in the social order, she is gradually brainwashed into accepting herself as a non-person with no rights or privileges to claim, no duties or functions to perform, no aim in life to achieve, no aptitudes to consult or fulfill.

That this is a grievously unjust state of affairs cannot be denied. It is unjust first and foremost to the blind woman herself. For what is a blind woman but a normal person who happens not to see? She has the same aptitudes and talents, the same gifts and abilities, the same potential or lack of it as any other human being in any cross-section of society. The only difference is that the blind woman uses her other senses to compensate for her lack of sight in carrying out her duties or in achieving her potential.

To deny her the achievement of this potential is surely a grievous loss not only to herself, but to the community and to humankind. If, in the teeth of discrimination and prejudice— without equality of advantage or opportunity, without the facilities for education or training—and by dint of sheer willpower and innate talent, blind womanhood can produce dedicated social workers and gifted authors and musicians; if blind women can make an appreciable mark in the field of education; if they can work in fields, factories and offices; if they can be brilliant students; if they can make significant contributions to the social life of their communities; then surely they can take their rightful place in the family and perform their natural role as wives and mothers, sisters and daughters. For, if blind women have proved that physical blindness does not confer a corresponding blindness of talent and ability, they have also shown that the inherent instinct of motherhood and homemaking is not dimmed or dulled by their disability. Blind men and women have met and married and proved that they can bring as much to the success of a marriage as can their sighted peers.

Like any other woman, the blind woman has the makings of a fine housewife and mother even without training and orientation. There are several examples of blind women who have been able to give expression to their abilities, without training or education, and are running model homes and bringing up fine children. Unfortunately the trend has been to regard them as exceptional and rare cases, verging on the miraculous. If the truth were known, I dare say, there might be many more such women living and doing and achieving, making their own silent contributions to their families and communities in obscurity.

But, on the other hand, how many countless others are living lives of quiet desperation and unwarranted deprivation, their talent unrecognized, their abilities dormant, their potential untapped? According to statistics there are approximately fifteen million blind people in the world today. However, it is likely that this figure falls far short of the actual. If accurate statistics from the developing countries were readily available, the real number would be nearer thirty million, of which fifteen million would be women. Most of the latter are likely to live in rural areas. Fifteen million lives are being lived in the darkness of despair, in the dystrophy of talent and ability. How many homes that could have been, how many lives, wasted lives, that might have been. If the sum total of all these wasted talents could be calculated, the loss incurred by society might surprise us all.

The time has come to set the balance right. In fact, it is long overdue. It is time to rescue blind women from their dreary dark corners, to bring into the light of day and the mainstream of useful, active life those thousands of blind females whose energies and talents are being blighted and sacrificed at the altar of ignorance and prejudice. It is time to restore to the blind woman her rightful role as wife and mother, and her rights and privileges as child, girl and woman.

How can this be achieved? What is needed is a down-to-earth scientific approach to the situation and its solution. The first step, which is of utmost importance, is for itinerant social workers to enter the homes where blind girls and adults are confined and then to re-educate parents, relatives, neighbours and the community and to break age-old misconceptions about, and attitudes to, blindness. This work has already started on a small scale in a few countries of Asia and Africa by some voluntary societies such as the White Bonnets Scheme of the Ghana Society for Blind Welfare. Established with the help of the Royal Commonwealth Society for the Welfare of the Blind, it is working with about 1,500 blind women throughout rural areas of Ghana, teaching them occupations and helping their integration into the community. However, what is needed is for the national governments to launch a comprehensive program, especially in small towns and villages of the developing regions, so that help reaches every blind girl and woman wherever she may be.

Simultaneously, blind girls should be allowed and encouraged, by all the national governments of the developing countries, to educate themselves. This should lead to a stage where education may be made compulsory for them in residential or integrated schools and colleges so that they can develop and grow mentally as normally and naturally as their sighted counterparts, and can equip themselves, not only for careers, but for enlightened motherhood and efficient homemaking as well.

Next, special training centres should be established in all the countries of the Third World, where blind girls can be trained to lead normal lives without sight, and where they can learn domestic science and the arts of homemaking and mothercraft. Here, mobility training should be given to enable them to move freely, gracefully and independently with the help of a cane. Typing, and reading and writing of braille, should be taught to ensure communication apart from educational activities with the sighted and other blind persons.

In rural areas, a woman is much more active not only at home, but in the fields where she works side-by-side with men. Thus, she is a great asset to the family and community. There is no reason why a blind woman cannot assume this role if she is given the opportunity and training. The training centres established in these areas should, therefore, include training facilities for agriculture, vegetable gardening, animal husbandry, poultry farming on a small scale and other rural crafts. These centres should encourage and invite visits from the general public and community to educate them in the abilities of blind women, so that the age-old distorted and incorrect concept about blindness is gradually removed. This will raise the value of blind women in marriage. Marriage is of supreme importance in the social/cultural patterns of rural communities and is the only way to give purpose and meaning to the life of a woman and the only means through which she can participate fully in family and community life. For most women in these regions, her most important and only career is marriage. A blind woman must be trained to ensure that she is equally, or more, efficient as a sighted woman.

A vast storehouse of potential lies waiting to be tapped. It is for us to seize the initiative, to make the effort to draw on the potential and to help it to flow into and merge with the mainstream of modern, liberated, active and useful womanhood.

INDEPENDENCE FROM SPOILING PARENTS
The Struggle of Women With Disabilities in Japan

Yukiko Oka Nakanishi
JAPAN

Father asked me
to take a bath.
I watched on TV
a baseball game.
His voice became
Louder and louder.
Father and mother
bathed me.
Father and mother
massaged me.
I thank you.

THIS IS A POEM written by Mr. Kuniharu Tanaka, a severely disabled wheelchair user in Japan. A volunteer opened a course on poetry writing for disabled youth to let them review their way of living, which had often been overprotected. Kuniharu realized through writing many poems that he had been indulged by his parents with too much love and care. He found out that the parents' hands with which he had been embraced, and the parents' backs on which he had been carried, were no longer big and wide. He recognized that parents grow older and he may not always have them with him. He is, thus, appreciative of their untiring efforts to physically care for him.

The parent-child relationship is very much closer in Japan than in other parts of the world. Since the family is united as one entity, parents treat a child as their own spiritual and physical part, as if a child was their belonging. Because of that relationship, a parent-child double suicide is an incident that is peculiar to Japan. The parent, in accompanying the child into death, often makes the excuse that he/she does not want the child to live a life of suffering without his/her assistance and support. If a child is disabled, public sympathy is expressed to the parent, who has no option but death to save the disabled child from future hardships. There is strong criticism raised by severely disabled persons against a society which so easily denies disabled children's right to live.

A meek, quiet personality in children, women and elderly persons is highly valued in Japan, while an explicit ego and an independent spirit in an individual member are considered negative elements in the family. The strong sense of kinship hinders these weak members of the family from developing an independent spirit. There is a clear distinction between inner society, where an individual can open him/herself as a member of a family, and an outer society where he/she is treated as a part of the labour force or as a member of the voiceless crowd.

Parents' love and control are more intensified in the case of a child with a disability. Paternalism is strengthened by fear and pity for the child's troublesome future. Parents feel a great sense of responsibility to protect the child as long as his or her life lasts. This is shown in patronizing attitudes, and the control is imposed more heavily on disabled girls. Society, in addition to having a preoccupation with the work-role of women as unpaid wives and mothers, and negative perceptions of the capabilities of women, considers disabled women to be second-class citizens. Parents, therefore, believe that a poor, dependent daughter should be fed all through her life.

Even though I was brought up in a middle-class family with well-educated and rather progressive parents, my experience tells me how limited are the opportunities given by parents to a disabled daughter. My parents did not force my sister and me to learn flower arrangement and tea ceremony. The acquisition of these traditional skills entitles a girl to get married to a man with prospects. Since my parents were different from ordinary parents—who provide their daughters with a good education and training to make them knowledgeable and skilled housewives, and who ask their relatives and friends to introduce their daughters to a man who has graduated from a first-class university—we were encouraged to pursue our studies at graduate school. I was treated in the same way as my sister. We studied at the same schools, though I needed an attendant to commute and to use the toilet at school. We were taken to theatres, museums and historical sites during vacations.

Discipline was rather strict, though, in order for my parents to bring us up according to their expectations. In the teaching of manners and social customs, the emphasis was on how to live harmoniously and obediently with others. There was often conflict with our parents, who forced us to follow the path set by them, before we could make up our own minds which course in life to choose. Their control over me was stronger than over my sister because they thought I had fewer options than she did. When I was interested in joining a broadcasting club in high school, they selected the art club for me with the hope that my hidden artistic potential might be developed.

Just before my university entrance exam, my father passed away. Mother's desire to make me economically self-reliant became much stronger, as she was faced with the difficulty of earning enough income to support the family. I was forced to major in English literature in order to obtain English proficiency for a career. My freedom was finally attained when I decided to stop working as a researcher at the university and moved to a newly-established organization, the Japan Council for the International Year of Disabled Persons. All of my energies were spent trying to convince her of the good in my actions. Since it was extremely difficult for disabled women to get good jobs, she wanted me to place priority on the financial security provided by the university, rather on a meaningful experience with fellow disabled persons.

Six years ago, Mother died, satisfied to see me working alongside able-bodied colleagues. I became financially and spiritually independent. I am appreciative of all she has given me, except my purely Japanese attitude. I become unnecessarily quiet and modest even now—even when working with other Westerners who are articulate and positive.

Many disabled persons try to escape from the custody imposed by their parents or, after the death of parents, by their brothers and sisters. Some of them have been trying to gain an independent life. The initial stage for independence is, in most cases, to leave the parents' house and to look for an apartment. The landlord is always reluctant to let a disabled person live alone in a rented room. In spite of difficulties at the very beginning, the independent living movement, especially among severely disabled persons and disabled women, is very active. The current interpretation of "independence" is not to merely obtain income-generating work for self-support, but, more broadly, it is to find a new self-determined lifestyle. The participation of severely disabled persons and disabled women has been spurring the development of this movement.

At the Asia/Pacific Regional Seminar on Women with Disabilities, organized by Disabled Peoples' International (DPI) in 1986, Ms. Keiko Higuchi, Vice Chairperson of DPI-Japan, reported on a new philosophy of independence for disabled persons. The independent living movement is ensured by the government's provision of pension, spending allowances and public assistance. Without earning a livelihood, disabled persons can achieve independence because they can determine their own way of life. However, she said that disabled women were treated only as disabled persons—their womanhood is completely neglected. They have to forget they are women in order to achieve independence. Expecting life to be a little easier, they even have their wombs removed. Mrs. T., who spent many years in an institution as a child and who now is living in the community, decided to have it done because she thought that life would be easier without her period.[1]

The Ichigo Association consists of severely physically disabled persons in Sapporo, a northern city in Japan. It aims to develop accessible public housing in the community as a means of achieving independence for disabled persons, under the slogan, "I went shopping by myself, I cooked by myself, and I ate by myself." It was started in 1977 by Ms. Michiko Osanai who has severe cerebral palsy. She questioned the petition made by parents of disabled children to the local government concerning the establishment of a residential rehabilitation centre. I believe the parents, like my parents, wanted their children to be self-reliant. But the option they chose, wrongly, was to allow their children limited independence through the physical security provided by an institution. Is that what disabled children wanted? Michiko decided to leave her parents and started to live alone in a private apartment.

My struggle for independence has been limited to the family. However, Michiko's fight has been developed as a movement, involving her friends with severe disabilities, the community and local governments. She is still fighting with a society that regards disabled persons as feeble objects of charity and pity.

It was hard for people with old values to accept the fact that she got married to a non-disabled man. He looks after her and a baby every day, except when volunteers come to help them. They receive financial aid based on the Daily Life Security Law, which is just enough to cover living expenses.

"Housework, which is almost universally known as the responsibility of women, not only is not reflected in labour force statistics, but is also not considered as work by families and sometimes even by women themselves, probably because it is unpaid."[2] Michiko's husband has been criticized for not having a job, and blamed for getting money from the government by those who still stick to the conventional view of the woman's role in the family. It is considered proper for the husband to work outside, while a wife takes responsibility for the household, including the raising of the children.

The lifestyle of women *has* been gradually changing. It is no longer the obligation of women to obey their parents before marriage, their husband after marriage, and a son after the husband's death. However, many vulnerable disabled women are still struggling with those who govern them. They are learning to organize themselves, to push through their demands for independence. Their numbers are increasing. However, there are still many barriers. The life of independent living for disabled persons takes a lot of volunteers' hands, as the community does not provide the daily assistance of homehelpers. The lack of volunteers and funds to support their movement often puts disabled persons in a situation where they break out in a greasy sweat because they are holding off the desire to go to the toilet or they are waiting, hungry, in a dark room. Still, a lot of women with disabilities have begun to follow the path prepared by pioneering disabled women like Michiko.

FOOTNOTES

1 Keiko Higuchi, "Report of the Present State in Japan," a paper presented at the DPI Asia/Pacific Regional Seminar on Women with Disabilities, Seoul, South Korea, October, 1986.
2 Nafis Sadik, "Integration of Women in Population and Development Programs," in *Asia/Pacific Population Journal*, Vol. 1, no. 3, (1986).

"THEY DON'T EVEN WANT TO TALK ABOUT IT"
Women with Leprosy Speak

Group of Women from the *Conselho Estadual para Assuntos da Pessoa Deficiente*
(co-ordinated by Cirley Motta, Ana Maria Morales Crespo, Akemy Ishikawa and Cintia Clausell)
BRAZIL

LEPROSY, OR HANSEN'S DISEASE, is still prevalent in Brazil and few people want to recognize its existence. Society is afraid of it and the medical profession seems to know little about recognizing its signs and diagnosing it. In this article, a social worker offers an explanation about leprosy and its symptoms, and three women tell their stories about living with leprosy.

—

Irani Rodrigues is a social worker in the Health Centre of Sao Bernardo (state of Sao Paulo). She also works with groups of people with leprosy. The following is her explanation of the disease:

The most common symptom is a white spot, lacking in sensitivity, on the skin. But it is important that the doctors are prepared to recognize the disease. Initially, Hansen's disease does not have any symptoms, but with its evolution it causes deformities and injures organs. It may begin with little spots on any part of the body.

The bacillus that causes the disease is a very common one in Brazilians, but eighty percent of the people are naturally resistant to it. People inherit their capacity to resist it, and the chance of contracting it or not depends on a person's degree of resistance. The latent period of the bacillus may be long—thus, there is difficulty in detecting the disease from the beginning, especially because in its first period of manifestation the patient has no pain. This is the indeterminate form of the disease, and it may or may not progress from this initial form of the disease. The evolution of the disease will depend on the resistance of the person. Some people, even without any treatment, are capable of destroying the bacillus. In its initial form (I) it may or may not be contagious. If the person's body is not capable of destroying the bacillus the disease may evolve into these forms:

1. T (tuberculoid)—not contagious. This is when the disease manifests itself by just a few spots. The organism is resistant to the bacillus and does not permit its reproduction.
2. V (from Virchow, Rudolf)—this is when the organism encounters little or almost no resistance, and the bacillus is permitted to evolve and attack the skin and organs violently. This is the contagious form of Hansen's disease. It is transmitted through the respiratory system or cuts and wounds in the skin.
3. In some cases, the disease may be type D (dimorphous), which carries characteristics of both types 1 and 2.

Roughly, these are the forms of the disease. In each form, there are different groups of characteristics. If it were possible to detect Hansen's Disease in its type 1 form, it would be completely eradicated in Brazil in about twenty years, even without a vaccine.

In Brazil today, however, Hansen's Disease is endemic, affecting more than one person in a thousand. It occurs on such a large scale due to poverty, lack of proper nourishment and hygiene, and because people do not know anything about it. If the life conditions of people do not improve, the situation will become even more critical.

In general, people who have the disease do not even know that they have it. They are potential transmitters, and unless detection methods improve there will always be a big number of people contracting the disease without being aware of it. By the time a person starts treatment, the leprosy is no longer contagious.

—

The following are the testimonies of three women disabled by the disease, who are being treated in the Health Centre of San Bernardo do Campo in the state of Sao Paulo.

Mrs. L., forty-two years old, is married and has one son who is eight years old. He was born after she had had many miscarriages. Mrs. L. found out very late in her life that her paralysis was due to leprosy. She tells us that several people in her family seem to have symptoms, but they refuse to go to the Health Centre.

MRS. L.:

My son is eight years old. When he was born, I already had the disease. I didn't know its name and I was never afraid. I wish everybody could go to the Health Centre to be treated, but simple, uneducated people don't go. I'm from a very small place in the interior of the state of Sao Paulo. Forty-two years ago, when I was born, it was just forests. I didn't go to school until I was twenty years old. I used to be a maid and I went to a Catholic school in the evening. My father was a very simple farm worker. We had to fight hard; we went through many difficulties. I worked in the fields. I worked in the house. I was never afraid of working—I've always worked.

When I was ten years old, my foot became weak. One of my sisters started to feel the same thing when she was seven years old; another one started to feel her leg become weak and her foot bescome twisted when she was eight years old. She went to the hospital in Sao Paulo and had her foot operated on, but it didn't help much. None of us were diagnosed as lepers. We were all treated as having paralysis. My mother also had the same problem, and I was diagnosed as having it too.

I was married in 1972 and used to live in another city. My husband is a good man. He does everything for me. He married me in spite of the paralysis.

Later on, when I was expecting a baby, some black spots started to show up and the doctor said it was leprosy. During another pregnancy, the spots came back and I suffered from lots of pain. I was pregnant seven times. I had several miscarriages and one of my babies was born dead. It was then that the real problem started. A long time went by until I got pregnant with the son I have today. I asked the doctor if there would be any problems for the baby and he guaranteed that there would not be. During the pregnancy the doctor said I needed to rest because my hips were kind of twisted. I remembered that when I was a child I had had an accident with a heavy piece of wood from a fence.

When I went to the hospital to deliver the baby, I told the doctor about the disease and he treated me well. It wasn't a natural birth, but a Caesarian, and I had to have some tests done in order to undergo the Caesarian. I told him that even when I cut myself it soon healed, and there was no problem.

I have never had any problems either with my husband or the family. Only in the neighbourhood, at times, someone will call me "crippled," and my boy stands up for me. He doesn't let anybody call me names.

I like to travel, to go far away. My husband used to drive a truck and we would go "out in the world." I don't have many problems with my hands. I sew. I like to watch TV and to talk. I love to talk. I rarely sit and do nothing because then I feel as if I'm dying.

I also have heart disease. I am under treatment. I can't stop taking medicines. I don't want to die; I want to live, enjoy life. My husband is seven years younger than I am. I have my boy. I'm always laughing. Even when there is a misunderstanding between my husband and me, I laugh, stroke his hair and soon everything is OK. I'm always in good temper.

Mrs. E., fifty years old, is single. There were six children in the family, four of whom had leprosy. Two of her brothers died and she and her eldest sister have been treated for years. They hide it from everyone.

MRS. E.:

Fifty years ago, when I was born, my brother had the disease and he was put in a special hospital for lepers. I think I've had the disease since I was seven years old, but mother wouldn't take me to the doctor because she was afraid I would have to be sent to the leprosarium. A person who worked there began to bring me medicines and I began to take them, without the direction of any doctor. Later on, some twenty years ago, I began to treat myself at the Health Centre.

I no longer have my parents. But my father used to be a bricklayer and my mother took care of the house. We were six children (three boys and three girls). Two of the boys had the disease and are already dead. I'm the youngest and I have it, and my oldest sister has it too. Only one brother and one sister don't have it.

I worked in an office, in records, and today I'm retired (it's been twenty years since I retired). I had many problems with pain before I retired. But today I work selling cosmetics. I walk on the streets normally, although it is not easy for me.

The disease is not a problem for me. But if anybody hears the word "leper," they run away because people don't know that if the person is being treated she doesn't transmit the disease.

Doctors, in general, are unacquainted with the problem of leprosy. It is necessary for the universities to give their medical students a better education. I went to the optometrist because the disease attacks the optical nerve, and I took a letter from my specialist with me. The optometrist got so scared he wanted to throw me out of his office.

I have problems with my feet and with my hands. I've already had three surgeries. But I do handicrafts normally—I knit and crochet.

It's very difficult to talk about the disease with the family. My family doesn't even want to talk about the subject and much less about people who have it. Take my oldest sister, who has the disease—she has six children and none of them has even had a check-up. She has children who are married and she panics over the idea that her daughter-in-law may find out about it. Once my sister had a very intricate test because of a problem with her nerves, but she was told nothing about the leprosy. She mentioned to me that she thinks she doesn't have it.

Of course, she doesn't even want to talk about it, but the doctors don't say anything about it either. And we end up not knowing if the doctors don't talk because they don't want to or because they don't know about the disease. I think the problem is that they don't know. That's the reason they don't find it and they don't talk about it. And that's why the medical courses should give doctors the opportunity to know about the disease. They should be able to diagnose it and lead the patient to the proper treatment. It is possible to get rid of the disease if you initiate the treatment soon enough.

I went out with a man for three years and I never had the courage to tell him about the leprosy. Therefore, I thought I shouldn't get married. I never had another boyfriend and I've decided it would be better to remain single and not have to talk about the disease with anyone. It is easier.

My house is always full of people. Relatives are always there and no one has ever caught the disease. I think it is because we have the disease under control, and as I have mentioned, when a person is under treatment she doesn't transmit it.

Mrs. M., fifty-two years old, is married and the mother of two children. She has been treated for six years, from the moment the disease was diagnosed. She tells us herself that she may have contracted the disease before she was twelve years old.

MRS. M:

I was born in the state of Minas Gerais, in a small town. I noticed two spots on my face and forehead when I was twelve years old, and my brothers used to say: "You're going to become white," (I'm a black woman). Every time I took a picture the spots would show and I didn't even like to be in the pictures anymore. Then they became darker and they grew bigger but I had no symptoms other than the spots. I used to have headaches and nausea. My mother sent my feces to be examined because she thought those spots could be caused by worms.

My father was a ploughman and had eleven children. My mother had problems with her intestines. My father was OK. He didn't feel anything. Only I have the disease, no one else.

I think I got it in the school. I stayed in the school, in another city, from seven to twelve years of age, and when I went back home I had the spot. I was fourteen when we moved to a small town in the state of Sao Paulo; it was then that the spot grew bigger and I had stronger headaches. Always I had stronger headaches. I worked as a maid after my mother and father died.

I got married and we had two children. I had a miscarriage during the third pregnancy due to high blood pressure. When my first child was born (he is eighteen years old today) I had a strong reaction and I wasn't able to open my left hand, so I had to take care of my baby using only my right hand. It was difficult to bathe him.

My husband took a vacation from his work and we went to the state of Parana to my mother-in-law's. She massaged my hand, we had prayers over it, and it worked. When I came back to Sao Paulo I was already able to open my hand, but it was smaller than the other one. It grew numb (dormant) and stiff, but I worked just the same.

Time went by, the children grew older, my husband did better financially and we built a small house, near the city of Sao Paulo. The headaches kept on tormenting me, though. Six years ago, my husband decided to add one more room to the house. In the midst of wood and nails and all the dirt, I stepped on a nail and hurt my foot. Then there was a scratch and another, and an open wound. I had three open wounds on my right foot and I could hardly walk. I used to wear slippers and because there was cement and lime all around the house, it was almost impossible to cure the wounds.

I went to see a doctor in a Social Security Centre and I had a nurse put a bandage around my foot (it wasn't a clean and well-kept place). They asked me to go there every day to change the bandage. One day, a friend of mine gave me the address of the Health Centre in Sao Bernando and since she worked there she made an appointment for me. It was then shown that I had Hansen's disease. As soon as my husband and my sons learned that I had the disease they thought I should start treatment. This happened six years ago. Nobody in my family had any idea about it, and none of my siblings had it.

I don't feel that people behave differently with me. I like to be around people. I like to walk, although I can't walk very much. I like to go visit my relatives in the interior.

I don't have a lot of money, but I travel whenever I can. I like it. I used to knit and crochet but I can't do it anymore, because it hurts very much. My hands are seriously injured.

I think everyone should have periodic checkups to be able to control the disease from the start. I belong to a group of lepers in the Health Centre and we are going to begin a campaign in the schools to call attention to the disease. It is amazing to realize that people are so ignorant about it. People get horrified just hearing about it. I think it's very important that this group go to schools and talk about Hansen's Disease. A child may alert the adults.

Also, the doctors should be better informed. They don't advise the patients. Take my case, for example—I've had the disease all my life, but I'm fifty years old now and I've only known about it for the last six years. Now I'm under treatment. If I had started the treatment before now, I would not have so many problems.

BANGLADESHI DISABLED WOMEN FIND HOPE

Bonita Janzen Friesen
BANGLADESH/CANADA

INTRODUCTION

The country of Bangladesh, situated in the Indian subcontinent, is a low-lying country, physically dominated by an extensive network of rivers that drain into the Bay of Bengal. It is a lush, beautiful land which supports more than one hundred million people within its small borders. The economy is largely based on agricultural production and the majority of the people are scattered throughout the countryside in small rural villages. Although the emerald greens and golden hues of the landscape provide a tranquil scene for the passing traveller, the people are not caught up in this natural beauty. They struggle with natural calamities and human selfishness in the competitive fight to feed their families.

Several major cities house masses of people, both rich and poor. Every day, rural people, who have lost possessions and land from natural disasters and unrelenting debt, move to these cities seeking labour or employment—a new way to survive. In the streets beggars roam their chosen territories, or sit on their mats in a strategic corner. They hound the passing population, beseeching them for handouts in the name of "Allah" (God), calling down blessings upon those who give a few coins. They curse the rich, who ask forgiveness for not giving.

People with disabilities who are also beggars are visible. Many aspects of their life stories are similar. From birth or accidental injury they have been destined to occupy a place at the fringe of society, resigned to their status as beggars. Physically disabled women among them are outwardly bold. Sometimes they display their contorted limbs or handicap in a way that will attract the pitying eyes of those who pass by. In a country where a woman's role is traditionally in the home, rearing children and remaining out of the public view, these women have had to shed the modesty of their rural, secluded lifestyle in order to survive the streets.

Still lower in status are mentally disabled women who have run away or, sometimes, been driven from the shelter of their home to scavenge off garbage heaps in towns and cities. The more fortunate of these women are sheltered in their own *"bari"* (homesite), where they are feared and allowed to roam as they wish. They may be largely ignored, but do not suffer the disgrace of public immodesty.

Some of these women are called *"pagul"* (crazy) and it is often unclear as to whether they have been mentally handicapped from birth or have had emotional breakdowns as adults. Even some physically disabled women acquire the term *"pagul"* when their communication patterns and behaviour deviate from the norm. If such a woman comes from a family who has had contact with her since childhood, the family may occasionally attempt to track her down and bring her back to the homesite. But if she is a little too aggressive or free-spirited she will soon slip away again to her uninhibited street life. She will scavenge for food and clothes, begging for a little food or money and sleeping in a street corner.

In the opinion of the mainstream Bangladeshi, severely physically and mentally handicapped women have few family options and almost no opportunities for employment. If a woman is married before incurring an injury or illness, her husband will likely divorce her, taking her children with him or giving them to someone else to raise. Attempts at rebuilding family life around a woman's disability are rare, since the Bangladeshi society has few built-in coping mechanisms to allow disabled women a place in the mainstream.

Poor physically disabled women may join a beggar community in a larger centre, where others will carry or push them to their chosen place of daily begging. They will probably have to give a cut of their "earnings" to those who help or who dominate the begging activity in that area.

There are very few institutions in the country that will house disabled persons or provide some kind of rehabilitation program that could steer these women towards acceptance in the larger society. Even destitute women *without* disabilities are rarely employed in visible types of work. Thus, those who are severely handicapped have no dreams of providing for themselves or even of being accepted as full citizens in the community. Often, disabled women resign themselves to the fate allowed by "Allah." Their life consists of looking out for themselves as they struggle to exist in a competitive society.

DISABLED WOMEN FINDING HOPE

There has been established at least one institution in the capital city, Dhaka, to address the physical, social, emotional and economic needs of paralyzed people in Bangladesh. It is called the Centre for the Rehabilitation of the Paralyzed (CRP). Valerie Taylor, a British physiotherapist, began this Centre in 1979. It remains the only one of its kind in the country.

Patients of the CRP are usually those paralyzed as a result of illness or accident. They stay an average of five months, during which time they will receive training in new skills that can be used to earn money. Ultimately, it is hoped that their training will prepare them for return to their home or employment and, as much as possible, to their normal lifestyle. I visited this Centre a few times to talk with some of the women who were there for training and physical therapy.

WOMEN AT CRP

As I sit in a circle with some of the women at the Centre I ask them about their lives and how they cope with their disabilities. Some are hesitant to reply. Kalpona Rani Das is a new patient from Borisal. She is adjusting to life at the Centre. She sits silently in her low-level wheelchair, or "trolley" and shyly avoids my questions.

Jobedha Begum tells of how she was paralyzed when a mud wall of her home collapsed on top of her, injuring her spine. Her baby boy survived the mishap without injury. She seems a happy person and smiles when she says that she does not know yet if her husband will divorce her. This is a likely possibility.

Some of the women seem to think that they have become paralyzed because of bad luck or because they have done something wrong. They talk together as though they belong in this life that fate has brought to them. Perhaps they have more joy and hope as they gain enthusiasm from each other. The CRP social workers keep in touch with them even after they leave the Centre. Thus, in spite of their loss of physical abilities, family members and a stable home environment, these women are a part of the CRP "family."

MOHUA PAUL

Mohua Paul is an attractive, energetic woman who is on the staff at CRP. She came to the Centre as a patient and therefore can relate to others who come for rehabilitation. She is the secretary and plays a vital role in the daily leadership of the CRP.

Mohua was paralyzed because of a spine disease when she was very young. She was lonely and often ill while living at home in Chittagong. After she came to the Centre she became involved in many activities. She plays guitar, cooks, sews, and embroiders jute. She has also travelled to various disabled persons' sports events and conferences in England, India and Pakistan.[1]

Mohua is from a middle-class family which was able to afford medical treatments to try to cure her. But after being in and out of several hospitals over a number of years, they had little hope. Her brother, a doctor, tried to help her, but with little success. So she stayed at home for eight years. Her mother and father heard about the CRP but were reluctant to send her, since she had often been sick at home in Chittagong.

Mohua told me, "I was depressed and didn't know my needs and was treated more as a child. I read books and wrote letters to the Centre social workers (who had been in contact with me) ... I really liked it when I came to this Centre. I realized there were others like me."

Mohua's friendship with one of her brothers who stayed in Dhaka helped her keep in touch with her family. She took accounting and secretarial skills training, since the staff recognized her skills in these areas.

In the future Mohua hopes to continue working with disabled people. She explained that she wants to do some volunteer work with the Bangladesh Disabled Association. In the meantime, Mohua seemed very caught up in her role at the CRP. "At home I was very alone and I was very sick. I have learned everything at the Centre. This is my life. I am very happy here."[2]

RASHEDA BEGUM

Rasheda is from the Dhaka area and has been in the CRP for rehabilitation a couple of times. She is paralyzed from the waist down, and yet is able to use her sewing and paperbag-making skills to provide some self-employment. She smiles quickly and is teased by some of the other women at the Centre. They coax her to tell me her story.

After her paralysis and while at the CRP, Rasheda received training and became actively involved with others. There she met another patient, Rohim, who worked in the workshop and she fell in love with him. Their romance, unusual because most marriages are arranged, led to marriage and they lived as a couple for awhile. But, as Rasheda explains: "in the end he left me for another wife." She had now returned to the Centre for an operation. She says, "I want to go back to my 'bari' (home) to live with my mother and brother. I will do some work at home—make paperbags to sell for the market ... I would like to leave the Centre, but my disability keeps me here now."

PEARA BEGUM

Peara spoke of a disabling disease that she has had for over eighteen years. Before her paralysis she was married, and she has one son. Then, because of her disability, her husband divorced her. With emotion, Peara explained that she lost her son of one-and-a-half years. The new wife of her husband had not wanted Peara's child and Peara suspected foul play. "But even with a case I would not be able to bring back my son," she wept.

In spite of her losses and increasing disabilities, Peara did return to her home in Lokhipur, Noakhali, where her parents live. She helped with the cooking, did embroidery and made fans for extra income. But after a period of sickness she returned to the CRP for further physical treatment. The staff at the Centre were working to find an organization that would shelter Peara for the long term. She explains, "I am afraid that I will be left alone if my parents die. My brother is still around, but he may not always care enough to help me."

HELEN MENDES

Far away from Dhaka and the women at the CRP lives Helen Mendes. She is thirty-two years old and has lived with her parents, Parcy and Selin, all her life. Her mental disability has kept her away from school, marriage and childbearing, which are a normal part of life for women of her age.

I went to the village of West Bodaripur in the southern district of Noakhali to talk with Helen. The Mendes are a Christian family and their home is situated in a rural Catholic community, close to the town of Sonapur and the church compound where they worship. Christians are a minority among the predominantly Muslim population. They tend to segregate themselves from the larger society to protect their own beliefs and practices. The Mendes are of middle-class status, owning some land and a beautiful homesite with a couple of bamboo and tin-roofed houses. Helen is their only daughter and their two sons live in Dhaka, working to provide the family with more income.

After making our way up the muddy path to the Mendes' home, Yvonne D'Silva, my contact, and I were warmly greeted by Helen's mother, Selin. We were ushered into the large central room of the house, out of the monsoon rain. There we met Helen and were asked to sit down for tea, as is customary in Bengali homes. Helen was all smiles and shyly took a seat at the table as I insisted on talking with her directly. With the help of my friend, Yvonne, I asked questions about her daily routine, her childhood and her dreams of the future. Because of her disability Helen has difficulty speaking, but she tried to answer my questions when she understood. Her mother, Selin, constantly interpreted my questions for Helen and tried to answer for her.

Selin did not know the exact cause of Helen's disability, but explained that she had been given some injections when she was pregnant with Helen. Then, as a newborn, Helen was very jaundiced and sick. After that, the problems began to appear. It took Helen seven years to learn to walk and she still has minor problems with co-ordination and lack of strength in her hands. She cannot do fine embroidery or sewing tasks but is able to do simple mending, cooking, cut meat and vegetables, and help with many household tasks. Helen's major disability seems to be her speech impediment, but she is able to communicate well with her parents and the other extended family members living on their compound. Her parents and others, who told me about Helen, considered her mentally disabled. But her disability and its cause have never been clearly diagnosed, according to her mother.

Selin happily tells of her love for Helen and how nice it is for her to be with them as they grow older. Yet, she expressed concern that others in their community cannot accept her daughter. When Helen was eight years old, her parents tried to send her to school in the "baby class" (kindergarten). But the other girls would tease her and she did not continue with school. Said Selin, "People ask why she can't talk since she is so old already. People don't understand why she is like this because there are few people like her that go out and about! But if she had received special teaching at an early age she could have learned well—maybe reading and writing." So, although Helen is perceived as being mentally disabled, her mother felt that Helen could have been challenged to learn more skills if she was accepted in the larger community.

When I was questioning Helen about marriage and encouraging her to tell me why she does not consider it, she became quite emotional in her embarrassment and frustration to explain. She rushed out of the room in tears after trying to say something. Her mother said that she wouldn't want to take a husband, because she could not communicate with him. In spite of their love for Helen, her parents do not see a future life for her, in marriage or employment, outside their home. For them, she remains as a child in need of protection.

As I talked with Helen, and returned for a second and third visit, I developed a feeling that her abilities had not been challenged. She seemed capable of more than she was doing at home, but she would probably never want to leave the acceptance and security of her family. I asked if she would consider working outside the home. She said that she would be interested if someone would be patient enough to show her simple tasks they needed to have done in their home. She could cook and clean for someone or take care of their children. Once, when in the capital city with her mother, Helen had helped with a cleaning job.

Since she smiled a lot and giggled with me at jokes, I asked Helen if she was always happy. She replied, "Usually ... at home, but there are frustrations ... get angry ... can't say what I want to." I asked what made her sad. "When know others are talking bad about me," she quietly mumbled.

Helen does go outside her home to church and to some school functions. She said, "Relatives who see me understand ... they know, but others ... I get shy, and upset ... go out—only with mother."

Helen's life is not complicated with questions of survival on a daily basis, as are the lives of other disabled women who have been cast out of their homes and family life. While her parents are able to shelter her, she will not be worried about her future. Yet, when I asked about this, she admitted that it is a concern. She turned to her mother, "What will I do when you die?" Selin answered, "Your brother or relatives will look out for you."

In conclusion, some disabled women in Bangladesh, such as Helen Mendes, live in a secure environment. Even disabled women like Mohua Paul at the CRP have some opportunities because their families can afford to pay for medical bills and they have contacts with people at larger centres. However, for the very poor women of the villages and cities who find themselves destitute and struggling to deal with their disabilities, there is little hope of life beyond the begging ring, far away from home and loved ones.

FOOTNOTES

1 Peter Hunt, "Centre for the Rehabilitation of the Paralyzed," *Jogajog Barta* (1988), p. 25.
2 Ibid, p. 26.

NETWORKS OF SUPPORT

Jayne C.M. Whyte
CANADA

SUITABLE SUPPORTS, BOTH INFORMAL and formal, are essential to overcoming or living with mental illness. To illustrate, I'd like to share the experiences of a friend I'll call "Eileen," as well as share some of my own story. Both Eileen and I are different from many others because a number of people around us really cared what happened to us, supported us in crisis, advocated for appropriate treatment, and gave us opportunities to succeed.

EILEEN'S STORY

Eileen was in tears. She had just returned from a trip to the city for a follow-up visit after one of her many hospitalizations for severe depression. "And so the psychiatrist said if I wasn't willing to leave my husband and kids, there's no use coming back to see him."

"What do you think?" I asked.

"I don't want to leave my husband. I won't leave my kids."

So Eileen and her husband went back to the family doctor for a referral to a different psychiatrist. Group therapy and the right anti-depressant gradually renewed her health. Fifteen years later, Eileen is working, helping to pay for her children's education, and living contentedly with the husband she was advised to leave.

In Eileen's case, the depression had a physical cause that could be relieved by the proper prescription, although it seemed like a setback when it took a period in hospital to find and adjust the medication. At the same time, she joined a self-help group where she met other women who had left jobs to care for children and were feeling left out, depressed, undervalued. The members of the group provided practical suggestions and moral support as she searched for and started a job.

Her new therapist encouraged her decision to seek part-time work, rather than reinforcing her duty to stay home or the disability created by her depression. Her husband had difficulty accepting Eileen's new assertiveness and independence but shared her determination to have a healthy personal life and marriage. Her new co-workers expected her to carry her responsibilities, but were accepting and supportive. And she found a trusted neighbour in her church who would look after her children while she worked.

This story sounds too good to be true, but what you don't see are the hours of agonizing conversation, the grim determination, and the moments of despair and panic that punctuated this process for more than a year. Nobody can say it was easy and there's no promise that Eileen and her family will all live happily ever after.

However, this story does illustrate the various components of a good mental health strategy.

The physical as well as emotional causes of the illness were recognized and treated appropriately. Some people reject the idea that psychiatric illness may need to be treated medically. In many cases, until the depression is alleviated, no amount of positive reinforcement can help the person change his/her life. Sometimes the cause is a physical imbalance; for example, manic depression that can be controlled with lithium. A complete checkup is also good medicine. One of my friends developed severe psychosis because tiredness was misdiagnosed as "nerves" instead of diabetes. When the doctor listens and believes the consumer as she sets out her hunches and fears, a partnership for health can develop.

Eileen set her own priorities—staying married, getting a job—and received encouragement and support in those decisions. Depression is often caused by feeling that we have no control over our lives. And when we've lost our self-esteem, others can remind us of our strength and value and of our right to live our own lives.

Fortunately, too, Eileen's family was not poor, and she had training that merely needed refreshing before she could get good employment. She started with only a few hours per week and increased the work time as her health improved and her children grew up. Her employment allowed the flexibility she wanted to attend the school functions that were important to her and her children. Such flexibility in the workplace is an exception, but more people, not only those recovering from mental illness, could benefit from tasks and hours that allowed them to balance their lives.

Poverty and lack of education and training, compounded by mental illness, keep many people feeling trapped, especially if they are also single parents, immigrants or living in isolation. Studies and recommendations about women and mental health must examine the whole social and economic basis of society—a topic too big for this article.

Therapists do not necessarily consider day-to-day difficulties and opportunities. Regaining the confidence to drive or learning bus schedules are not part of the material covered in "life-skills training." Building a career wardrobe on a welfare budget is not an easy task, even if you are on good terms with the thrift shop. Good childcare is a concern for many mothers. Yet who thinks of these as "mental health issues?"

The self-help group reduced Eileen's sense of isolation and assisted with problem-solving in her daily life at home and at work. Because she did not live in the city, she drove more than 200 kilometres round trip to participate in the weekly group. And if she phoned her therapist or another group member during the week, her long distance bill increased. "But," Eileen emphasized, "if I were in the hospital in the city, I'd be phoning home, and it's better to be home." Her family agreed.

Eileen's husband often shook his head as his wife made progress then became ill again, but he remained faithful and encouraged her efforts. He found that he needed help in understanding and accepting her new attitudes and demands. His idea that he should work to support her and the children and she should stay home and look after him was challenged. Regaining health can be as hard on a marriage as years of illness, because roles and expectations change.

As Eileen gained confidence in sharing her feelings with her therapist and the group, she began to trust herself to go to church and participate in a mid-week Bible study. Acceptance by people who reflected the love of God was another step in restoring her self-image. And it was a member of that group who said, "I'll look after your pre-schooler and the other two girls can come after school," when Eileen needed a babysitter.

MY EXPERIENCE

My experiences are similar to Eileen's except that my marriage couldn't withstand the pressures of my changing health. I moved to Winnipeg when my marriage ended because the therapist I needed worked here. It has been hard to leave my son with his father in Saskatchewan, but with the right help I am getting well. A friend believed that appropriate treatment was available, and kept searching until she found a mental health team that could help me.

One of the mental health dilemmas facing women is that we are taught always to be unselfish. Giving myself permission to look after *me* has been a struggle. I slowly came to realize that I have a right to ask for, and hope of getting, what I need.

Members of the Canadian Mental Health Association (CMHA) became my friends and valued my perspective as a consumer of mental health services. CMHA has developed a "Framework for Support" model which points out that the person with the problem is also the centre of her own support system. All too often, the professional, the hospital, the well-meaning relative, or someone else seems to take control away from the individual who has been labelled mentally ill. And as I said before, depression is caused or aggravated by a sense of loss of control.

But the person is not expected to go it alone. Family and friends are the first people most of us turn to when we are troubled, lonely, or sad. Often, just talking things over with someone we trust is enough to help us regain a sense of perspective and purpose. Family and friends are also essential to people who face severe psychiatric disability.

Over the years, I have learned to maintain a group of special friends that I have recruited to provide extra support at crisis times in my life. I have explained my illness, and how they can help, informed them of the professionals who can be contacted if necessary, and reassured them that they have a right to say "No," if I ask for help at an inconvenient time. I try to keep at least three such contacts within walking distance, and make sure they know who else is in my network, so that we all feel safer.

Moving to the city of Winnipeg from a small community meant a period of time where this network of friends broke down. And the Crisis line has become part of my network, as close as the telephone, especially in the middle of the night.

When the problem is too big, we need the resources of the formal mental health system. It is now nine months since I was last hospitalized. For me, that is a long time to be home, especially when I am also adapting to a new community, marital separation, and starting work. I owe a debt of gratitude to the mental health team who have been therapists and supporters. I especially appreciate their willingness to let me work towards my own objectives, and their respect of my knowledge of myself.

Through the church, the Canadian Mental Health Association, and my part-time work, I am gradually rebuilding a community of friends and special friends. Community organizations, agencies, and employment are important aspects of the personal support network. I am also part of a group of people who experience the same diagnosis as mine and we help each other by sharing— not only through words, but through practical tasks like moving furniture and having fun together.

My objective for myself has always been to enjoy a full and useful life with appropriate support when I need help.

There are many aspects of the mental health system and society that need reform. I choose to work through the Canadian Mental Health Association to create change. But one of the most powerful tools is for people to tell their own stories of pain and success. The experience we have gained by surviving must be shared with the professionals and the decision-makers to create a healthier world for all of us.

Best wishes as you build your own personal networks of support and as you teach what you are learning.

II

OUR IMAGE IN THE COMMUNITY

Many people, including the disabled, still believe the traditional myths about the disabled. Some of these negative attitudes have their origins in ancient religious beliefs that regarded the disabled as devil possessed, or as corporeal manifestations of family guilt. These prejudices have been buttressed by fear, particularly of the able-bodied, that their own good health might be a temporary state, that they too could be suddenly struck down by an accident, disease or the effects of age, or that through association with the disabled, a condition could be "catching."

— Pat Israel and Cathy McPherson
("Introduction," in *Voices From the Shadows*, Gwyneth Ferguson Matthews. Toronto: Women's Press, 1983, p. 14.)

WOMEN WITH DISABILITIES HAVE experienced many attitudinal barriers to being accepted in the community as contributors like everyone else. All the women in this section describe how people's attitudes have limited their participation, and that of other disabled women.

Juliana Abena Owusu and Rosallie B. Bukumunhe describe traditional attitudes towards women with disabilities in Ghana and Uganda respectively. They describe how disabled persons are seen as a shame on the family. Both Juliana and Rosallie emphasize that the coming of Europeans to their countries meant changes for disabled people—schools and training opportunities opened up, and Rosallie was offered corrective surgery and an education by the missionaries. They also emphasize that disabled persons' and disabled women's groups have offered disabled women empowerment and a way to effect change.

Eileen Giron of El Salvador writes that women with disabilities in Latin America have difficulties finding employment and in forming loving sexual relationships. She writes as a middle-class woman who achieved a high level of education, and yet could not find a job due to discrimination. Eileen describes how disabled women have banded together to start sharing their struggles.

Susan Gray and Judith A. Snow, both from Canada, explain that attitudes in the community have caused tension in their pursuit of independent lives. Susan reports that her hidden disability and its limitations are not readily apparent to people and therefore they often do not understand her inability to perform certain tasks. Judith A. Snow explains that the rigid attitudes and schedules of institutional life almost cost her life and her ability to work and support herself. She then recounts how she and her supporters formed a network to break her out of the institution and allow her to live in the community.

All the women who, like Judith, tell their stories in this chapter, continue to empower themselves in the community, despite the barriers and pressures they describe.

STRUGGLE OF DISABLED WOMEN IN GHANA

Juliana Abena Owusu
GHANA

IN THE PAST, MANY people thought that the only places for women were in marriage and childbearing, in the kitchen and in the tilling of the land. The general situation of women in developing countries is not encouraging. Despite their importance and massive contribution in various fields of life, no due recognition has been given to women by Ghanaian society. But, in reality, women play a pivotal role in the family and in the process of socialization of the young.

When the government rehabilitation program started in 1960, it was discovered that there were no fewer than 100,000 people in Ghana who were disabled. The figure of 100,000 includes 10,000 children, and eighty percent of these handicapped persons were in the rural areas with no formal education or training, and no means of earning a decent income. Without the establishment of some special facilities for rehabilitation and education, they were prevented from participating effectively in the economic and social life of the country.

It was also discovered that the major causes of disablement in Ghana were onchocerciasis, or river blindness, and polio. It was, therefore, recommended that the control of onchocerciasis be intensified and children be innoculated against polio. (John Wilson Committee Report, 1960). Ghana's total population (1984 population census) is twelve million and a little over half of the total is represented by women. Over thirty-one percent of the total population live in the urban areas and almost sixty-nine percent live in the rural areas. It is estimated that about five percent of the population is disabled (the statistics on disabled persons are not up-to-date). Ghana is a heterogeneous society and the culture varies from one tribe to another, and from clan to clan.

For centuries, women's competence has been seen as inferior to men's competence. This concept of women has persisted up to this day and women have been made to believe this. As a result, women have been, and are continuing to be, exploited and under-rated. An example is the woman who goes to the farm with her husband and participates fully in the farm activities. After a hard day's work, the tired wife has to carry a headload of firewood and foodstuffs, and then double that load by carrying a child on her back, while the husband idly follows at her heels, whistling to himself. At home, the man goes out to play drafts (a variation of chess) and gossips over palm wine while the woman prepares food and goes about all the household chores before satisfying her husband's sexual demands in the night.

Gone, however, are the days when certain jobs and professions were looked upon as the preserve of men and thereby labelled "for men only." In Ghana today long distance heavy truck-driving is now a common job for women. In the urban areas, many women have risen to the top in professions and in business. A few successful women are placed in higher positions—they are administrators, doctors, lawyers, lecturers and industrialists. But rural women are far behind their urban counterparts in education and employment because the majority of them are illiterate. They are mainly peasant farmers with small land holdings, petty traders, dressmakers and craftspersons. Some of them are unemployed or have to be content with carrying loads in the market for small fees.

Ghana's history is replete with roles played by women. Noteworthy of mention is Yaa Asantewaa, the queenmother of Ejisu in Ashanti, who in the face of British colonial strength, rallied men and led an army in 1900. History has it that Ashanti, because of the exile of their King Agyemang Prempeh I to the Seychelles Islands in the Indian Ocean in 1896, had no leaders. Had it not been for the effective leadership role taken on by Yaa Asantewaa, who took to guns when the men were afraid, Ashanti would have lost the golden stool (the chief's throne) and its authority to the British. (*Ghana History for Primary Schools, Book 2,* E.A. Addy, pp. 56-58, and oral history).

In national disasters it is the women who have suffered most. In 1983, when about a million Ghanaians in Nigeria were deported, women had to carry their luggage and children throughout the ordeal. Some were pregnant and at the point of labour but had to sleep in open unhygienic places before their arrival in Ghana. I witnessed these experiences when I worked at one of the reception centres set up by the government to receive the deported people.

In famine and war, women are saddled with physical and emotional strains. Finding food, losing children to hunger and husbands and brothers to death, and just bearing the daily anxieties of life, became sometimes heartbreaking.

The situation of disabled women in the community reflects the situation of women in general. Both disabled women and men fall behind their non-disabled counterparts because they have for a long time been denied the opportunity to prove what they are capable of doing.

Throughout the ages in Ghana and Africa, disabled persons have been regarded with little appreciation. It has been erroneously assumed that disabled people are incapable of engaging themselves in any useful occupation, and therefore should be objects of sympathy and pity. Others considered disabled persons to be "sick," thus encouraging a life of confinement or privacy in the home rather than participation in work and normal community activities.

In both the rural and urban areas, disabled people are kept in dark corners of the village huts and houses, and have few opportunities to contribute to the life of the community. Disabled persons are left in houses to take charge of keys or to take care of children or to take mental notes of who comes in and out, while their non-disabled counterparts go out farming or conducting business.

In Ghana, as in other African countries generally, the extended family system has always been responsible for disabled persons, orphans and the deprived. But industrialization and urbanization are eroding the ability of individual members of the extended family to continue to provide this kind of support. The extended family is giving way to the conjugal family. In this situation, where parents are wage-earners working away from home, and the non-disabled children attend school, the disabled child or adult is left to fend for him or herself.

There is more acceptance for disabled persons in rural areas. This is because, in most countries, traditional norms do not permit people to neglect their disabled relatives. They fear that when they neglect disabled persons they will be punished by their ancestors. Disability was looked upon as an evil visitation, and the family supposedly was being punished for the perpetration of some evil. The disability was also considered a disgrace in a family, especially when it was congenital. The arrival of a disabled child into a family was to a large extent considered as a bad omen and the child was quickly done away with and hurriedly buried with the excuse that it had died at birth. For example, in the past, the cerebral palsied child, called "asuoba" (meaning the child of the river spirit) would be given back to the river, where it supposedly belonged.

On the other hand, some disabled children were considered lucky and were overprotected. Children born with large heads and fat cheeks were considered symbols of wealth and wisdom, nullifying all misfortunes of the entire family. If the family mistreated the so-called "sacrifice" child, it would be punished by the gods. If the family treated the child well, family business would flourish (oral tradition, also from Nana Kwasi Amonor of Kokofu—one of the historic towns in Ghana).

With these beliefs and attitudes, therefore, it is not surprising that in Ghana and in most African countries, the disabled persons were taken care of by the extended family and scarcely ever came into the open. They were often relegated to the back alleys of village huts and houses.

The few daring disabled persons who braved the situation and came forward succeeded only as beggars and had to travel long distances to practise their trades. Disabled people didn't like the idea of begging, themselves, but they are forced into it even today for the following reasons:

1. After being shut off in villages and homes for long periods without skills training and education, freedom in the streets means "begging" to them.
2. Some families do not provide for their needs.

3. Skilled disabled people cannot practise their trades because of lack of tools and materials with which to work.
4. Out of religious beliefs, some non-disabled persons encourage beggars, especially as a way of fulfilling their religious obligations to give to the poor and unfortunate.

The total impact of all this on disabled persons is lack of proper supports, because there is no fear of the wrath of ancestors in the urban areas.

When disabled women are alone in the house, those with severe disabilities are tempted, wooed and flirted with by the opposite sex. But men deny paternity when the women become pregnant. This affects those in the rural areas more than those in the urban areas.

In the early 1950s, voluntary organizations, individuals, and Christian missions concerned themselves with the care of disabled persons, mainly the blind and the deaf. Special schools, like the Akropong-Akwapim school for the Blind and the Mampong Akwapim School for the Deaf, were set up. Both schools were established in rural areas. A workshop was also opened in Accra by the Ghana Society for the Blind (then the Gold Coast Society for the Blind). It has taught blind women in both urban and rural areas handicrafts like doormat-making, soap-making, home management etc. This system has served over 6,000 blind women and men and it is still working (Records of the Department of Social Welfare).

There are no reliable statistics on the total number of disabled persons which the system served, but, according to the available information, when it was realized that the problem had become so enormous that government involvement was needed to make it work better, the government did step in. As a result of the John Wilson Committee Report of 1960, a division of rehabilitation was set up within the already existing government department of Social Welfare and Community Development. The Committee stressed that if no special provision was made for the education, training and rehabilitation of the estimated 100,000 disabled persons in the country, they would be prevented from effectively participating in economic and social life.

Based on the recommendations of the same report, an industrial rehabilitation centre was established in Accra to give a short intensive course designed to build confidence and teach basic skills. The centre not only provides vocational training, but it provides the conditioning process which is required before most disabled people can undertake specific training for employment. In addition, eight other rehabilitation centres were established in other regions of the country which also teach disabled people handicrafts such as cane-work, shoe-making and repairing, farming, dressmaking and tailoring.

Non-governmental organizations are also working to better the lives of disabled persons. The Ghana Society of the Physically Disabled, of which I am an executive member, acts as a pressure group, and through press education and publicity it is helping to eradicate the situation. Through the Society's efforts, disabled persons enjoy free rides on all government-run transportation systems, with the exception of air travel. It has also established, with the assistance of the Norwegian Association of the Disabled, the Jachie Training Centre, which offers vocational training and resettlement to both disabled women and men. This supplements government rehabilitation efforts. As well, the Society is still working tirelessly to improve attitudes and beliefs towards disabled persons.

There still exists prejudice and misunderstanding in the community about disabled women, and disabled people in general. In some cases, these prejudices are even associated with taboos. For example, in some areas both blind women and men are not permitted to enter the chief's palace and sacred groves on festive occasions. In 1981, the Chief of Fomena in the Adansi District in the Ashanti Region refused to welcome a government delegation led by the late Isaiah Boakye, himself blind and a former tutor of Obuasi Secondary Technical School, because of his disability. Secondly, in 1982 when the king of Ashanti, a province in Ghana, passed through the Edwinase Rehabilitation Centre to the Kwasdaso Agricultural College on a visit, he directed that all the blind students of the centre be kept indoors because a traditional ruler must not see the blind.

As for education, there is a great lack of training facilities for the blind and deaf persons who need special education. There are only two elementary schools for blind people and only two secondary schools which have departments for blind students. All three universities in Ghana have limited training opportunities for blind students.

There are ten elementary schools and other unit schools (integrated into the main school system) in the country. There is only one secondary technical school for deaf people at Mampong Akwapim, and one vocational training centre at Bechem. Physically disabled persons who need no special education also face a number of difficulties—such as architectural barriers. For example, about four years ago, a female student, Miss Comfort Serwaa Sey, who was reading a degree course in Land Economy at the University of Science and Technology in Kumasi, became physically disabled through a motor accident and was forced to abandon her course due to architectural barriers. A male disabled student of the same university had to change his major from chemical engineering to social science for the same reason. Traditionally, parents also tend to educate their disabled boys more than girls. Yet, when given the opportunity, some disabled women have risen in commerce, industry, business, government, and education.

Another struggle is employment. Employers tend to emphasize handicap more than ability and ask questions like, "What can she accomplish? Can a disabled woman manage a job?" There is also heavy stereotyping, which results in restricting disabled persons to typewriting and sedentary office work. Given the right training and environment, the disabled woman is sometimes more efficient and hardworking than her non-disabled counterpart. I am proud to say that I work to the satisfaction of my employers, who admire my work.

My busy schedule includes registration of disabled clients, referring of clients to appropriate quarters for the solution of their problems—for example, the Ministries of Health, Education and Labour for medical rehabilitation, special education and employment respectively; and rehabilitation institutions for vocational rehabilitation. I counsel clients on their problems. In addition, I do field work such as resettlement and follow-up work on students who passed out of the rehabilitation centre in my region

(Edwinase Rehabilitation Centre). I also handle welfare cases such as child and family maintenance.

The disabled woman's struggle also takes place in the social arena. The disabled woman who is able to push herself into social activities like watching football matches and attending dances is greeted by casual but injurious remarks like, "What do you want from here? You should pity yourself," and so on, merely because she limps on one leg or is blind or deaf, or walks on all fours (a "crawler"). Miss Helena Owusu, who walks on all fours, had just such a nasty experience at Hotel de Kingsway, when she attended a dance in Kumasi three years ago. Both male and female trainees of the Edwenase Rehabilitation Centre experienced the same thing in May 1980 at the Kumasi Sports Stadium, during the Papal Mass Celebration by His Holiness Pope John Paul II. There are also architectural barriers which prevent disabled persons from participating in indoor social activities.

Marriage is another problem for disabled women and men because of traditional beliefs and prejudices in the community. In Ghana, and in most African countries, marriage is not simply a union between a man and a woman, but an alliance between two families or what we call a group of kins. Marriage is an alliance in that it is a union or joining together of families. According to custom, one's family can refuse permission for a member to marry a particular person because of his or her disability. A man and a woman cannot marry without the consent of their individual families. In some areas, the man's family has the right to choose a partner for him.

It is also by marriage that a child is given a social status and is established in the community as a socially responsible member. Marriage is, therefore, an integral force in the community and it invokes strong feelings in the general public. It is integral because a family is brought into being through marriage and dissolves through death. Without the birth of new people, society will die out. Marriage is therefore the basic social unit through which society is created.

In some cases, unless the disabled woman is beautiful, highly educated, or fabulously rich, she encounters marriage problems and is, at times, forced to remain unmarried. This affects disabled men, too, because marriage to a disabled woman is often discouraged by families for fear that they will give birth to disabled children who will be a shame to the family.

A good example is provided by the case of Nana Kwaayie, a Chief (traditional ruler, real name and town withheld) whose marriage to a deaf woman had to be broken because of threats from his people, who were bent on destooling him for marrying a disabled person. (Chiefs in Ghana sit on stools and not on thrones. They are, therefore, enstooled and destooled.) In addition, many men deny paternity of children they have with disabled women through concubinage, especially when the disability is severe, because of peer and family pressures. Insinuations like, "Why did you choose a disabled woman for a wife when there are still so many strong and beautiful women in this world?" are often pronounced. This has resulted in many single-parent families for disabled women in the country. In the rural areas, disabled women are made to marry men who are less important, just to bear children for the family.

The following are some suggestions and recommendations for improving the welfare of disabled women in the community:

1. The government must implement awareness programs for the public and specific target groups so that women with disabilities will be viewed from a positive and dignified perspective. This will help erase the rather erroneous impression that disabled persons should be seen as objects of pity and as liabilities and misfits, who can only sit on the roadside and beg for alms.
2. In the developing, as well as industrial countries, it is the people who are the basis of development. Therefore, both disabled women and men must also be recognized as essential resources.
3. It is only through integration that disabled women can hope to accomplish the highest level of independence for themselves. Barriers are sometimes put in their way, making it impossible for them to move about as freely and as frequently as they might wish to. For example, few people will sit with them in buses and lorries. The integration of disabled women into community life must be seen as the most important factor in the rehabilitation process.

4. The negative societal reaction that accompanies the marriage of a disabled woman must be eradicated, to avoid the stigma disabled women bear by giving birth to illegitimate children.

5. Disabled women should free themselves from the shackles of their disability. They should transcend all barriers—physical, artificial and psychological—and fight for social equality. They must prove to the public that, given the necessary training and the right environment, they also can contribute to the community in which they live. Physical disability is not necessarily a liability or handicap. Disabled women must form pressure groups to press for more rights.

6. Disabled people in general must be given equal opportunity to receive education and training, through the provision of free access to all educational institutions and also to all public places.

7. Measures to vaccinate against commmunicable diseases, such as polio and onchocercasis, must be intensified. Speech therapy, physiotherapy and prosthesis fitting centres should be provided in all the government hospitals. Information must reach those in the rural areas, since a higher percentage of the population live there.

8. Finally, the public must be educated not to pity or assist disabled women by giving them alms only. Society should change its negative attitudes towards disabled persons and encourage them to acquire a trade, skills and an education. This will enable disabled people to live independent lives and to contribute to the community. It is necessary to teach a person how to fish, rather than giving her a fish for just one day.

The Ghana Society of the Physically Disabled and the Ghana Federation of Disabled are working hard, through press conferences, mass media, and organized talks in churches, to eradicate negative attitudes. I am also trying my best to organize disabled women to come together and to fight against the situation ourselves, because "she who wears the shoe knows where it pinches."

As a famous Ghanaian philosopher, Dr. J.E.K. Aggrey, aptly said, "If you educate a man you educate an individual, and if you educate a woman you educate the whole nation." As a follow-up to this wise statement, I would like to add that, "if you educate a disabled woman, you educate a community."

ON LIFE WITH AN INVISIBLE DISABILITY

Susan Gray
CANADA

I WAS BORN WITH a physical disability—a bleeding disorder which manifests itself in an extreme shortage of platelets and severely impaired platelet function. In short, my blood has a very poor ability to clot. The presence of this disability is extremely difficult for the public to detect. Other than bruises (which are usually hidden by clothing), it is impossible to tell that I have any disability. I don't use a wheelchair, my speech is clear and my arms strong—I have a classic invisible disability.

The presence of an invisible disability has created a paradox in my life. I am strong enough and co-ordinated enough to do anything from slicing apples to riding my bicycle across town, from climbing a mountain to having a baby. And yet, my participation in each of these activities is overshadowed by one ominous sanction: "Go ahead and do what you want ... just don't have an accident!" I can't afford to get hurt when a cut can result in a blood transfusion, and a broken bone could be fatal. My abilities, then, are wide in scope, but the restriction imposed by my disability is, at once, tangible and intangible, concrete and nebulous. "Don't cut yourself!" is hardly abstract! However, whether or not slicing an apple will cause me to cut myself is nebulous indeed. Who knows? Who cares?

I often find myself saying, "Who cares?" This brings me to a second point in my discussion of life with an invisible disability. One might think the fact that this phenomenon is hidden from the world is a fortunate thing for me—that people necessarily react to me, rather than to the disability. After all, I don't look outwardly different, at least not the kind of "different" that attracts stares running the gamut from patronizing to curious. When someone rushes to hold open a door for me, I know it isn't because I appear unable to manage said door on my own. And yet, other people's reactions to my disability and its accompanying limitations or restrictions are probably the most confounding part of the whole disability!

Meet Nan and Fran. I've been working in the office with these two for about four months now. Nan is a born athlete, a born organizer and she is a woman who knows what she wants. She's also hugely suspicious because, although I run two-and-a-half miles a day, I never participate in our office intramural football games (which she loudly organizes). These games are supposed to be crucial to ... to what? ... hell if I know, but this kind of pressure makes me feel so guilty, I feel like inviting the whole team over for lunch during half-time. Now, Nan knows I feel guilty, and this used to prompt her to keep pushing me to play. Lately she's changed her tack and merely bounces by me with the players list, putting her arm around people, telling them, in her booming voice, how great it is to have them on staff and how their participation in intramural football really shows their commitment to our organization.

I don't know, but I think I've kind of started to hate Nan. Maybe what I really hate is the fact that I've explained about one hundred times that I cannot play contact sports with this disability. And every time I explain this, she looks me up and down (ever so fleetingly), raises an eyebrow to her friend Fran, silently says, "You are lazy, over-dramatic and selfish," and bounces loudly away (no one bounces as loudly as Nan).

Fran usually remains standing in challenge after such a scene. She, too, is suspicious of this whole "bleeding disability" business and periodically attacks me with some form of innuendo. I always know when it's coming. She kind of bends forward, lowers her head and looks up at me with those mean little peepers. And then it's always something like, "So—I have to find staff who can slice fruit and cheese for our annual general meeting. I know you haven't been—er—able to help out with this in the past, but I thought I'd at least try one more time—I really hate asking the same people who've helped out the last twenty-five times." Now what do I do? Do I look down at my strong well-coordinated hands and say, "Sorry Fran, I'm not supposed to be doing much slicing?" Or do I become totally intimidated and change the topic and blather on and on about serving lunch to our office's intramural football team next weekend? Or do I just slice the damn food and hope I don't get cut? The choice is mine. Oh yes, my friends, *vive le libre choix*! Some free choice! And always I ask myself, "Am I shirking my responsibilities? Is this disability controlling my life?"

Now enter another great paradox. Sometimes my life with an invisible disability is affected, interestingly, in the opposite way. Many people around me, because they cannot see the effects of "Glanzmann's Thrombasthenia," are terrified of it. They dread being the "cause" of something happening to me. The more controlling of them dread the guilt they would experience if they were to "allow" me to do something that would result in my bleeding. These people do everything short of throwing cloaks across water puddles so that I may pass with dry feet. They walk the city streets with me, poised, ready to leap screaming in front of oncoming traffic. They have the damnedest way of grabbing my scarf to pull me back at crosswalks while *they* check for traffic. This can be most irritating. Their reactions are usually born of true concern—how can I get angry at people who care so much? When does their caring become control? Why does their caring so often make me want to go out and work in a knife factory?

My disability does present the odd benefit, however. Hey! Who really wants to bounce around the football field under Nan's sweaty arm at eight a.m. on a Sunday? I can't play football, and every Sunday morning (when I wake up for a few blissful seconds to realize I can roll over and sleep under warm soft blankets for another three hours), I thank God for that sad, sad fact.

TOWARDS INDEPENDENCE

Eileen Giron
EL SALVADOR

EL SALVADOR IS THE SMALLEST country in Central America, and it is also the most crowded. It is located on the Pacific coast and the neighbouring countries are: Guatemala, Honduras and Nicaragua. The main cause of disability is malnutrition. No one has ever tried to do any statistics on the number of disabled persons. It could be from eleven to thirteen percent of the population.

I was born in a small town, close to the border with Guatemala. I had polio at the age of twenty months and was left almost a quadraplegic (paralyzed in four limbs) as a result of it. I went to a regular school and, by coincidence, out of five children, I was the only one in the family that never attended a Catholic school. After some years I was able to understand how good this had been for me. Nuns and priests were always telling me, "You have to be patient. God loves you very much, and that is why you are suffering now." And I always felt uncomfortable in their presence.

I remember how happy I was when I was really young. The town was so small that there was no need to have a car to go anywhere. We had a good position in town—my father is a medical doctor and mother has always been involved in community activities.

After finishing primary school, I wanted to continue school, but there was no place I could go because the buildings were totally inaccessible. So I decided to take private lessons on the subjects that I enjoyed the best, which were foreign languages and painting. For my parents, whatever I decided was fine with them as long as it kept me busy.

When I reached adolescence, I started to have some concerns regarding my self-image. There were so many thoughts coming to my mind, such as, "Why am I different from the others?" The worst thing for me was not having anyone with whom I could share all my concerns. Sometimes I would burst into tears without any specific reason. I could never explain what was going on with me, not even to myself.

My oldest sister and I had a group of friends that was always together. I was the only disabled person in the group. We were always going to parties. For me, these were always opportunities to meet someone who could be my boyfriend, but boys were never interested in me in that way.

We never had any kind of information regarding sexuality, not even regarding our own bodies. We were curious to know, but were always afraid to ask. I remember asking my mother the meaning of the word "masturbation." Her answer was that good girls should not talk about that. It took years for me to understand the real meaning of it.

My sister and girlfriends married when they were very young and my world changed—I didn't have a group anymore. Since I had always been interested in art, I went to an art school in another city. For the first time in my life I met a man who was interested in me as a person. He was a foreigner. I fell in love with him, but I was convinced no one could ever love me. We stayed very good friends for a long time.

During all this time the self-help movement of disabled persons did not exist for me. I didn't even like to be with other disabled people—but this didn't mean that I didn't have any problems because of my disability. My problems were always with my mother, who treated me like a child. I always had an attendant, but when my mother had to help me I felt really miserable. Actually, now our relationship is much better, but we do not live together any longer.

I started to make plans to go to Europe and spend some time there. It was like an impossible dream—that was all I could think about for two years, and many letters were sent before I could find an accessible place to live and to go to school. I looked for an attendant and finally I was ready to leave.

TOWARDS INDEPENDENCE

Germany was the first step. I was so happy—I'd made it. Then came Italy and France; Europe was mine. I loved the cities, the people, the food, everything—I loved the personality I developed away from my family. I was me. Except for a broken leg, I never had any serious problems.

After two years, it was time to settle down. I wanted to work. I came back to my country, full of enthusiasm, proud of myself. I never doubted that I would easily find a job—there were not that many people who could speak three foreign languages fluently.

Looking in the newspapers for job announcements and making phone calls turned out to be a routine. I had many interviews, and people could not help being surprised looking at me for the first time. Tired and frustrated of filling out so many forms, I decided to give language lessons for children. I put an announcement in the newspapers, but when parents found out that I was disabled, they did not want to send their children to me. Finally I became aware that although I had changed, things at home, like prejudices against disabled persons, were still the same.

THE GENERAL SITUATION OF DISABLED WOMEN

Being a woman in a Latin American country is already a handicap—women have hardly any time to learn to read and write since they start at a very early age to do housework. These are women from the low income group, which is the majority. They don't have many work opportunities, except to become a servant or a prostitute.

Severely disabled women with low incomes almost always remain at home. They never go to school. Their families consider them sick persons. Even if they are not severely disabled, in some cases they are not allowed to do anything. They are completely dependent on others to do things for them. For example, a woman who is forty-four years old and is a quadraplegic as a result of polio, has never been outside the city without her mother. She has never been in a supermarket or a bank. She just visits some friends once in a while. A twenty-six-year-old hearing-impaired teacher for deaf children went to school in the United States and was living in a dormitory there. Back home in El Salvador she lives with her parents and her mother takes her to work every day. And if she wants to go somewhere she has to ask permission and be taken by one of her younger sisters. She says that she gets really bored with her family, but does not know how to be totally independent. In some other cases, disabled women are exploited by their own family, because they have to do all the housework and do not have any chance to live their own life.

In the rehabilitation facilities, disabled women are taught to sew, but when they go back home they can't afford to buy a sewing machine. And there is no way to buy a machine except to place an announcement in the newspapers requesting the help of a generous person to obtain it.

Blind women find more job opportunities than most disabled women. They work in factories as telephone operators. They also work in gymnasiums as masseuses.

For middle-class women the situation has improved a lot. After finishing school, many go to college and work at the same time in order to obtain better life situations. But, for most disabled women, things are still the same. In most cases, the family is overprotective and women never have a chance to live independently.

Maybe not being able to live independently is one of the many reasons why disabled women never get married. They never have a chance to meet anyone, and if they do meet someone, they lack the privacy to develop any kind of relationship. The poor self-image that most disabled women have does not encourage men to have anything to do with them. But perhaps the most important reason why disabled women don't get married is that in our culture men are educated to be served by women. In general, men will never think of sharing their lives with a disabled woman. Many of them are even ashamed of being in public places with a woman who is not attractive, from their point of view. They also view disabled women as asexual beings and this is an important factor in disabled women not becoming involved in sexual relationships.

Blind and deaf women, respectively, do not have as many problems finding a sexual partner—they usually have their relationships with blind men and deaf men. It is still difficult, however, to have a permanent relationship.

INVOLVEMENT OF DISABLED WOMEN
IN THE SELF-HELP MOVEMENT

When the self-help movement in the United States was already obtaining victories such as access to public transportation and access to public buildings, a few disabled people in El Salvador began to get together to start a self-help organization. In eleven years, the number of disabled persons active in the movement has not increased in the same proportion as the number of disabled persons. This means that even though there are many more disabled people now, there are not that many disabled persons involved in the movement.

The philosophy of the self-help movement is not fully understood yet. But what is important is that there are already a few leaders who are totally aware of the importance of the movement. They are working hard with grassroots organizations and starting new ones. Among these leaders are some women and they are very effective. In fact, disabled women started meeting in their own group in January 1987. Little by little they are beginning to be aware that they have some right to decide things for themselves—they have the right to be wrong and the right to learn from their own experience. They are getting involved in the self-help movement, but it will take some time until they understand what the philosophy is really about. When this day comes, problems will still be the same, of course, but there will be the strength, not only of one woman, but of many women together talking for ourselves.

"I Will Definitely Go"

Rosallie B. Bukumunhe
UGANDA

DISABILITY IN UGANDA, a developing country in the centre of Africa, is as old as time itself, I believe! There are legends of lame warriors, stories of one-breasted and one-armed witches in many parts of the country. There is also a popular and interesting story of an ugly hunchback who, by taking the place of a bride, outwitted an unkind gorilla.

In the past, disability was largely a result of ignorance in society. The standards for hygiene were very poor. Children born in a state of disability were treated in very bad hygienic conditions which brought no change, for even the so-called medicines were prepared and stored in dirty places. And when no better results were seen after the use of medicines, most people resigned themselves to fate. They concluded, "It is God's wish." They resorted to sacrifices to appease the punisher—either God, or the devil—because the parents had done something they should not have done or left undone something they ought to have done. But even this did not improve matters.

In the past in Uganda, disabled persons, men or women, were a great inconvenience to their families, their relatives, their villages and to themselves. Some disabled people were seen by others as able to do nothing, apart from talking and eating. There were some disabled persons who were not severely disabled, but even they needed a lot of help. They could not go out to bring water from the well for themselves; they could not go to find food for themselves from the garden; and they could not go to the forest and bring home firewood.

The country had many tribal wars and a number of man-eating animals. So to leave a disabled person alone was, in some cases, a great risk. It was, therefore, necessary to leave another person in the home all the time to take care of the disabled person, or alternatively, to carry the disabled child wherever one went. This was very inconvenient because walking was the only means of transportion at the time. There were no bicycles, no motorcars, no buses, no trains. To have to be a disabled person was almost a curse! The disabled person hated it and other people hated it too. So a disabled baby in the home became a great social problem in the family. The relatives who would, in other cases, rejoice and congratulate the mother on having a baby, instead came to mourn with the mother.

As well, friends in the village would not bother to come. If and when they came, the mother would hesitate to show her baby, as is the custom. Couples would then ask themselves, "Should we go in for another child or not? Perhaps the next child might be the same!" They were at a crossroads, especially the mothers, for fathers were normally polygamists who were sure of having or having had already, some able children from other wives.

To be born or become disabled was definitely worse for a female than a male. And this was so firstly and largely because females in Uganda did (and many still do) occupy a low social status. Females also outnumbered males in the population. So their problems were much more pronounced than those of men.

THE COMING OF EUROPEANS

Around 1900, Europeans entered Uganda. We are told that some came to trade or find markets for their products. Others say that they came to lead people here to God—the all-powerful God they themselves believed in. Whatever they came for is not very important. The important thing is that they found Uganda to be, by their standards, at a very low level of understanding about disability. They found people in Uganda to be very poor and illiterate; and they found disabled persons in the state we have so far talked about. The groups—the missionaries from the Church Missionary Society (the Anglican Church) and the Roman Catholic Church—immediately concerned themselves with telling Ugandans about God. They also wanted to improve health and life conditions and to make Ugandans literate. They used various methods to achieve their aims but largely they used the method of living with and among the people. They wanted to, and did, watch and study traditions, customs and sometimes the languages, and most of them left Uganda fluent in local languages.

Ugandans did not fear them—they made friends with them. But, as was the custom, it was usually the male Ugandans who came forward first, for it was the male who was the Chief of the village and all the councillors were also male. In addition, males would come forward to help these Europeans carry their properties on long journeys, and often worked as porters or houseboys. It was the male who was brave and did not fear strangers. Consequently, male Ugandans knew the Europeans well and made friends. The women, able or disabled, were not easily seen or met at first.

When the Europeans introduced things they gave them to the men and in turn the males introduced them to the women. But already men had patronizing attitudes towards women, so the good things did not reach the women immediately. The men believed that the women were not so deserving as they.

The European missionaries began to visit individual homes, wanting to meet even the wives and children. They invited the women and children to their churches and won them to their faith. They began to meet disabled people, the men first and then the women. The missionaries showed them love and gave them material help, too. The missionaries had made a breakthrough in showing people how Uganda was a big society. People began to meet and mix with others. This big society opened the eyes of Ugandans. People now knew that they were many—they learned that they were more than a village. More disabled people were discovered and they took heart. The Europeans told people that they did not have disabled children because the Creator hated them, nor had they offended Him in any way. They told the people that something could be done to change things. Missionaries encouraged people to take good and clean medicines which could even treat babies in the womb, and to bring forward all the disabled children to be treated and cured. Some people believed quickly and others took their time.

Here, I will give myself as an example: I was born disabled and my disability was particularly in the right foot, which had an arch that faced upwards instead of downwards. This is what my mother told me. Very late in the 1940s, on a certain Sunday of one month I cannot remember now, my mother and I went for prayers because she was a very keen member of the church and a Warden of our local Anglican church. As soon as we reached the church compound, we saw two European ladies who came from a certain boarding school, and they were missionaries as well as teachers. In fact, one of them was a headmistress of that boarding school. They were Miss Mary Mance and Miss T. Gerda. When they saw me they pitied me, and they held some discussions with my mother, who was also keen about my future. They suggested that I should go to school and that later I should go to the hospital and have an operation on my disability. Without hesitation, my mother agreed. She told me that I would be taken to school and have my foot operated on. I had only one answer, "I will definitely go."

When we finished prayers, I was taken to the car, which was ready to go. I was told to sit in the backseat with my new guardians, the missionary teachers. I had no property. The only thing I had in life at that time was the dress I wore. I was firm enough and asked my mother when I would be back. She answered that I need not be back, but the only thing which mattered for me was to get better, start walking and then start schooling. From such encouragement I developed some anxiety and wondered when we would leave. So, after some talking to other ladies at the church, the missionary ladies asked the driver to start the engine. And I had to say "'bye" to my mother, who was my only remaining parent, as my father had died long ago.

While in the car, the conversation went well because my guardians, the missionaries, knew many words of my local language. The journey took thirty minutes, as it was only twelve miles from my place to the boarding school. Monday, the next day, I started school, and I was very happy to be in the class, although I was a bit older than the usual P.I. level kids. I was glad to raise my hand during question times, though I often did not give the right answer.

After a year, I went to the next grade, and that was the year I was taken to a mission hospital, known as Namirembe Hospital, where I was operated on. I am sorry I cannot remember the name of my doctor, but he managed to turn my foot into the right position while I was under anesthetic. I saw it several hours later, when I came back to life. Although I was in great pain, I was happy to see my foot wrapped in plaster. It was almost in the same position as the other foot, though it was smaller. After three months, I was sent back to school with crutches and I was trying to walk on both feet just like a beginner. Three months later, I was taken back to the hospital for the removal of the plaster, which resulted in my present standing position. I was still limping, but at least I was better, and I felt very proud because by then I could wear shoes. I left the crutches, and started another life of doing all the jobs I could not do before, and I became serious about my studies up to my Primary Leaving Examination, which I went through very successfully. I went to a nearby Senior Secondary School up to the "C" level Standard, and then I joined a commercial school, known as the Uganda College of Commerce ("Nakawa"). I took the stenographer course for two years, and I was posted to the Ministry of Labour. After two years, I joined a co-operative bank—the Farmers' Bank—and I still work there today.

I am very thankful to those two missionary ladies who picked me up and brought me to the state where I am now. I can look after myself, though my parents have died. I regard the missionary ladies as my true parents. Once again, they were good. They were really very good to me—even now our relationship is close to that of mother and child.

UGANDA DISABLED WOMEN'S ASSOCIATION

In 1986, I became a member of the Uganda Disabled Women's Association. Although there were only a few members at first, I am glad to report that we now have 94 members in the Association. The Association was formed for disabled women to "work together to uplift the well-being of disabled women in Uganda." It was also formed to advocate for and to protect the rights of disabled women, as well as to work towards self-reliance among disabled women. Its membership is open to all women with disabilities regardless of their tribe or religion. And wives of disabled men can be members but cannot vote.

When we meet we do handicrafts of all types from our local materials. We make mats to sit on, baskets, trays, teapot covers, shopping bags, lamp shades, bedcovers and pillow cases. We also make saucepan stands from the tops of soda and beer bottles. Name it, and we make it here. We meet on the second Saturday of every month and then a member of the Association is allowed to bring her own handicrafts to be sold in the Association. And a member gives one quarter of what she makes to the Association.

We hope to open small branches in the country districts. We have already appointed one development worker who will be going around mobilizing disabled women to be more active in our Association.

Not only do we see ourselves as disabled, we are women. And thus, on March 8, 1988, the International Women's Day, we participated in marching through the city roads up to the Conference Centre. It was fantastic! Our speed was slow, but we enjoyed ourselves. We were cheered and encouraged by thousands of people to continue to the end. There was an exhibition after the marching where our handicrafts were exhibited and were snapped up like hotcakes.

Thus, disabled women in Uganda are overcoming centuries of prejudice, ignorance and of being hidden away. We are joining together and building self-reliance.

LIVING AT HOME

Judith A. Snow
CANADA

FOUR YEARS AGO I moved into my own apartment at York University with my own cadre of personal attendants. This step was both a major change in my own life and a major political victory for those Canadian citizens who are labelled handicapped. I would like to outline the story in this paper so that others can use my accomplishment as a model if they so desire.

I was born in October 1949 to an ordinary couple in the city of Oshawa. These people had had two ordinary children before my birth and would have another ordinary child when I was two. Only two things made my family particularly remarkable: one is that I was born with an unusually and severely limited use of my own limbs. The second, more significant difference, about my family is that my parents believed in my potential to be useful to myself and to my community. They believed I should have a chance to fulfill my potential.

Their belief in my potential as a human being marked my life and my family's career from that early moment. Society did not believe in the potential of citizens with severe handicaps. Therefore, my parents were quickly initiated into the red tape, inefficiency, short-sightedness and occasional maliciousness of the service structure that is supposed to meet the needs of people like me. We soon grew to know that we could expect little help and much bad advice.

My parents realized that I could and needed to contribute to ordinary peer relationships and experiences in my growing years. They knew that I needed a good education to open options for me as I approached adulthood. Consequently, we drove many miles, fought with several school superintendents and moved twice so that I could have opportunities to learn and play with ordinary school mates. My family also made or purchased my own special devices, and generally put in an extraordinary amount of time, energy and money.

Two years before I was ready for university, my parents took on the Vocational Rehabilitation Branch of the Ontario Ministry of Community and Social Services. We won a grant to hire an attendant who would provide for my physical needs at the university. Two months before my nineteenth birthday, I became an independently living adult in student residence at York University. Within the year I recognized that there would be no support for the cost of my attendant care when I graduated from university. I recognized that institutional life was awaiting me when I completed my student days. Other handicapped people and I banded together at that point to encourage the development of community-based services for people with physical handicaps. Along with others, I worked on the Kellerman House Committee and the Clarendon Foundation. Partly because of my efforts, new services were funded, but always for people with relatively mild handicaps. Those of us interested in the participation of citizens with severe handicaps were thwarted at every turn.

In April 1976 I completed my Master of Arts program, lost my funding for attendant care and entered a nursing home. For me and my family, this represented a defeat of our entire effort to support me as a contributing citizen.

During the following three-and-one-half years, I was forced to move from a nursing home to first one, and then another, chronic care hospital. The stated reason for this destabilizing journey was that the nursing home was unable to provide more than two-and-a-half hours of actual care in the day. I am a person who needs a minimum of five hours a day of attendant care. During these three-and-one-half years, in order to maintain my sanity and my interest in the outside world, I continued to work four days a week at York University. The money I earned was used up in paying for a semi-private room, a private nurse in the mornings and my transportation.

I needed a semi-private room because patients in a ward room often get little sleep as beds are changed during the night, people are turned, medications are administered. If you stay in bed all day, a short night's sleep is of no consequence, but I needed to sleep since I was going to work. I needed my own nurse, since hospital routine would not allow staff to get me up before ten in the morning. In fact, I was breaking the law by working at all, since disabled people who are funded in hospitals are by definition unemployable. The Province of Ontario could have cut the hospital's funding for me because of my employment, but fortunately they turned a blind eye to this. Also, the staff were always overworked and were glad for the hours when I was not around.

Near the end of the three years, two significant events happened. First, I met Marsha Forest and we became fast friends as we worked together on a planning committee for a conference called "Labelled Disabled." Marsha would invite me to speak to her classes of student teachers who were going into Special Education. Many knew nothing about people with handicaps and Marsha wanted me to tell them the real story.

The second event was that my health began to break down because of the institution, its policies, atmosphere and staff. No matter how hard I worked to explain how I needed to be active, I was always pushing against the life of the institution. After a time they would not let me have a private nurse in the mornings, saying that they could get me up in time for work. However, the staff soon resented my continuous need to be up quickly and early. When I returned each day, it was a battle to get to go to the bathroom, or to get my own supper, as half the staff were on their own break, and the other two had fifteen people in their beds to wash and turn and change in a forty-five-minute time period. The pressure on me mounted. The staff tried to get me to stay home, to stay in bed, to give up. Even in my semi-private room, the elderly lady in the bed next to me called "nurse, nurse, nurse" in her sleep all night. Under the stress of little sleep and constant hostility, I began to break down physically and emotionally.

In the summer of 1979, I fell ill enough to be moved to a general hospital. Doctors there found that I was suffering from malnutrition and bronchitis. Both of these conditions arose because my schedule conflicted with the hospital schedule. Often staff did not have the time to feed me my supper when I came home from work, or to take me to the bathroom more than twice a day. I was used to getting cold meals that had been sitting around for hours. Malnutrition saps your willpower, and I realized that I had not been fighting back hard enough, and that I would have to fight harder if I wanted to live.

The doctors and social workers at the general hospital looked for another way to get attendant care for me, but even they had to settle for sending me back to the chronic care institution. There were no new services for people needing more than two-and-a-half hours of attendant care. I returned ready to do battle for my life but my extra efforts to get more appropriate service from the staff made them resent me more. In retaliation, I frequently was assigned a nurse who did not speak English or one who treated me roughly. Marsha supported me in the realization that I was going to lose the battle for my life if I did not get out.

In October 1979, I left the institution to move into the hallway of a friend's apartment at York University.

When I left, I obtained a small grant from the March of Dimes to help subsidize my attendant care. I paid for the rest of my attendant care and my living expenses with my own money. I had a letter from the Province of Ontario saying that they were developing a service system of apartments with attendants for the people in the apartments, and that I would be one of the first to move in. I figured I could get by for the six months until this project opened. In the meantime, Marsha was introducing me to many new people such as Peter Dill, and showing them that I had something to offer as a teacher, a consultant, a friend and more.

In January 1980, the new apartment service informed me that I needed too much attendant care for their service, and that I was not going to be one of their new residents. I was left exhausted financially, emotionally and physically. I toughed it out for about two more months and then collapsed one day in Peter Dill's office.

Peter and Marsha took me to Marsha's house where I stayed for six days. During this time, Marsha called together fourteen people who knew me, and asked them what they were prepared to do in order to get me going again. I did not attend the first meeting, as I was not talking. I have attended all the others since then. The group decided that I needed my own place to live, money for the attendant care, someone to co-ordinate the schedule, and ultimately a governmental decision that would permanently fund my special services. Peter found me my own apartment at York within days, and a new volunteer, Sandy Gray, who co-ordinated my attendants and did some of the attendant care herself for the first five weeks. Later we would hire a full-time co-ordinator. Another Peter raised a loan from the York University Student Council to pay for several months of attendant care.

Then we all sat down to figure out how we could break through the government's prejudicial policies.

Four years later, I am still living in my own apartment with my own attendant care program which is fully funded by the Province of Ontario. The story of the political breakthrough, and the story of the development of an attendant care program that allows me to work and travel across the country is essentially the story of the Joshua Committee.

Nobody realized it at the time, but Marsha Forest and Peter Dill made history when they formed a support group around me to meet my needs as a person who experiences severe prejudice in Canada. The group started with fourteen people and is now a permanent lifetime commitment for Peter Dill, Marsha Forest, Peter Clutterbuck, Sandy Gray, Krista Chiu, Jack Pearpoint and Judith Snow. As we worked together to create a system that would meet my needs, we were developing a strategy that allows the government, the volunteer community sector and the person who needs services to work together for their mutual advantage.

The Joshua Committee began its work when we made the decision that I as an individual had been dropped through the cracks of the bureaucracy too often. We struggled with the decision that I deserved a support group of my own. As concerned citizens we thought that it might be too selfish to support just one person. However, my life hung in the balance still, and we all agreed that I could not afford to be dropped even one more time. We set out to break down the barriers facing me, and that is the reason for the name "Joshua Committee." We began to take on the walls of Jericho.

The wall, for me, is the government's policy against giving money to the individual who needs special services. For years I had been able to document that a private attendant care program was less expensive and more efficient than a group arrangement funded through an agency. For years I and others had known that institutional services kill people. These facts meant nothing to the

Province of Ontario as they could not see the logic of funding individuals and not agencies.

Ordinary citizens are very able to understand these facts. Ordinary citizens are not in favour of killing people, nor having their taxes wasted to do it. Marsha Forest organized hundreds of ordinary citizens behind my story to ensure that the Province of Ontario would listen. In addition, we invited Cabinet Ministers and senior civil servants from a number of relevant Ministries to come and see my apartment, to eat lunch with me, and to talk to the people who were hired as my attendants. Not many came to lunch, but those who did were impressed. We gained the ear of the Cabinet, and less than two months after my collapse I had my own private attendant care program.

This crumbling of the wall of Jericho is a history-making event. Since my first contract was signed, approximately twelve other people who needed attendant care have obtained government funding for their own programs. This is the good news. The not-so-good news is that the Province of Ontario still refuses to give money to individuals, and still will not make the provision of individual attendant care into a policy of the Ministry. This means that each individual must find an agency who will accept the government money. In turn the agency gives it back to the individual. This also means that all of the private programs now in existence are written as Orders-in-Council, directly from the Cabinet level. This is an expensive and time-consuming process for everyone, but the government still cannot see the wisdom of giving money to individuals.

The model of personal support that I have is unique and, we believe, worthy of being copied. I have a group of attendants, two full-time and three part-time, and several volunteers. Three people provide a twenty-four-hour program for me that can go anywhere in the world. The people who advocate for me, help plan and design modifications, and who provide support to my staff are the Joshua Committee. These people are all volunteers, and only Krista Chiu is also an attendant. Frontier College, whose President is Jack Pearpoint, provides the funnel for the money. Then the government provides the money itself, which makes my full participation possible. We have shown that the individual, the volunteer sector, agencies and the government can work effectively together if the volunteer level receives respect and cooperation from the other levels, and if the individual is also respected and listened to.

At the moment I no longer have an attendant care co-ordinator. We found that an adequate attendant care program, respect and a relationship with the community were the ingredients to spark major personal change for me. Since the beginning of the Joshua Committee I have changed jobs, moved, and changed in many other ways. As I became more active, and particularly as I began to consult across the country and in the United States, no co-ordinator was able to know where I would be next. Consequently, I now do my own scheduling, payroll, training and the hiring and firing in conjunction with another Joshua member.

Our work together has taught us and others several new things. We have learned that systems of special service can and should be developed around individuals. We have learned that a properly developed service system can compensate for a person's handicap and, literally, unhandicap that person. I still cannot use my arms and legs, but I can live and work in a normal and contributing manner. We have learned that a community can exercise real responsibility for a member who is handicapped, and do so in a way that enhances that person's own responsibility to themselves and to the community. We have learned that the private individual, the professional and the person with special needs can work together. We also learned that this service can be provided at a significant cost-saving to the taxpayer. My present attendant care system greatly enhances my life, my work, my friendships and other relationships. The service costs approximately thirty percent less than what the death-dealing institutional system charges to own me.

I offer my story with the hope that I can communicate a new way of thinking about people with handicaps, and about providing service. We cannot continue to force people with handicaps away from their own homes, families and friends with the excuse that we cannot meet their needs in any other way.

III

IMPRINTING OUR IMAGE ON THE WORLD

My mother always said, "If you aim at the sky you might land on a tree." But, so what?

— Joyce Joseph *Trinidad and Tobago*
(Spoken at the Disabled Women in Development Leadership Training Seminar, in Roseau, Dominica, July 1988, sponsored by Disabled Peoples' International.)

WHETHER WOMEN ARE ARTISTS, writers or administrators, their issues are the same: they want to exercise their creativity on the world; they want to make their unique mark. Disabled women hold jobs or do their life's work in the community in almost every vocational category. The women with disabilities in this section share their imprints.

Joyce Joseph of Trinidad and Tobago tells of educating herself mostly at home and of learning how to sew. This eventually led to her own dressmaking business where she is sharing her skills with other women. Eunice Fiorito of the USA discusses what it was like to grow up as a blind girl, and how she was encouraged to pursue the career of her choice. She traces her educational and work experiences as an administrator and tells of how she has experienced more discrimination because of her gender than because of her disability.

Zhang Li recalls her childhood in China and the barriers she experienced in receiving an education. She was placed in an institution when her mother was unable to support her at home.

Zhang Li explains that her experiences in the institution were positive and she relates how she taught herself to read and write. And thus, she fulfilled her dream of becoming a writer.

zana's (United States) drawing "dance" reveals a woman in motion in celebration of life. Ventura Emma of Italy also discusses her experiences in a hospital as a young child. They were devastating for her and becoming a writer frees her to imprint her passion on the world.

Mikiko Misono tells of a discriminatory employment system in Japan which left her searching for old newspapers and bottles to support herself. And due to her own efforts she began working as a housekeeper. In the end, she bands together with a group of disabled women to offer classes in flower arrangement and English.

Mikiko Misono is like all the writers in this section who have, with talent and determination, imprinted their images on the world.

THERE IS A WAY!

Joyce Joseph
TRINIDAD AND TOBAGO

I WAS BORN ON the tenth day of the fourth month in the year 1936 to average working-class parents. My mother stayed at home to care for her family while my father worked at different jobs to provide for us. I am the fourth in a line of six children—one boy and five girls. Although we were not well off, we always had basic things like food, clothes and good shelter. Our parents took great care to provide these amenities for us. They were always there when we needed them.

In 1937, nine months after my birth, I contracted the dreaded illness poliomyelitis, in one of the worst outbreaks to hit Trinidad. I was later informed that quite a number of children had died. However, like myself, a number of children were left with varying degrees of disability. In my case, both legs were affected and my right foot was turned in, making it impossible for me to walk or put on shoes. At first I got around the house by dragging myself on my buttocks. Then as I grew older, I was able to hold on to the walls and furniture and move around.

At three-and-a-half years of age, I was taken to a pre-school where basic reading and writing for infants were taught. I was taken to school in a "go-cart" which was specially made for infants. I travelled in this cart past the age for which it was designed. In those days, transportation was not easily available and my family did not own a vehicle of any kind. This was a problem which my family was not equipped to handle and so my formal schooling ended at the age of seven.

My mother made another attempt to have my education continued—she arranged to have a teacher tutor me at our house, one evening per week for one hour. This lasted a little over a year and then the teacher moved away to another area. This brought my formal education to an end. However, I had a love for books. So I read with my brother and sisters, and also read anything I could lay my hands on.

I was allowed to do whatever I wanted to around the house—cleaning, washing dishes, dusting, needlework, etc. My elder sister was involved in needlework and sewing and so I got interested in these activities.

When I was about twelve years of age, a Canadian missionary who was working in Trinidad at that time became involved in meeting children with disabilities in various areas of the country. He was introduced to me and began visiting our home regularly. He became a friend to me and my family. This friendship was a stepping stone for me, as he got me interested in a class for children with disabilities that was started by the Red Cross Centre in South Trinidad. We learned to make craft items such as soft toys and also to knit and to crochet items. It was also an opportunity to socialize with other disabled persons. This was exciting for me and the others because this class allowed us to be able to get away from home, where we spent most of our days, and to mix with other persons.

The class continued for about three years and eventually came to an end. By then good friendships were formed and skills learned. At this time, my father, who was involved in community work, began a Youth Club in our house. I then had another opportunity to meet young people, and other friendships were formed. Some of them are still part of my lasting "list of friends."

In my teen years, I began feeling very conscious of myself as a person with a disability. As I look back, I can safely say that was the hardest period of my life. I had a number of good friends, both male and female, and I had a caring family, but I was very unhappy. To use a popular expression, I was "young and restless." I was afraid of the boys who tried to be close to me and felt that they wanted to make fun of me. I began sulking a lot and my mother could not understand why; she thought I was ill, and after a while, when nothing would stop my sulking, she took me to our family doctor. He could not find anything physically wrong with me. However, being a wise old man, he knew I was feeling depressed because I was not able to do what the rest of the crowd was doing. He suggested that I should see an orthopedic surgeon.

My parents had, in my early years, tried every doctor they had heard of to get help for me, but without success. However, they were willing to try once more and I was more than willing, as I saw this as a chance to walk and do some of the things I had wanted to do for a long time. I did see the surgeon, was admitted to the hospital in 1958, and spent eleven months having continuous surgery. My dream of walking with the assistance of only a cane never came true. But I was now able to put on shoes, walk with the aid of crutches and go out on my own without a member of my family.

For me this was the beginning of living. And while I was in hospital, I met a Methodist minister who used to visit the hospital regularly to see the members of the Methodist church. My mother was a Methodist and so he came to visit me. He was, indeed, a friend and he helped me to build self-confidence and my faith in God. I made a decision there and then to become a Christian and a member of the Methodist faith. This decision was one of the best I ever made. Through my church involvement, I have come to gain a personal knowledge of God and this is my secret for coping with my disability.

I was a member of a Girls' League which offered opportunities for training in Bible studies and self-improvement in general. Through my involvement in this group, an opportunity to travel arose. My self-confidence was growing because of my involvement with people of different backgrounds. Soon after, I began working with children and then the Youth Group and Sunday School. I did not feel as though I could lead any of these groups. However, the response and support I received helped me. I can now say that when God calls, He equips, and the personal growth I received from these experiences is unbelievable.

I am, at present, Superintendent of our Sunday school, leader of the youth class, president of the women's fellowship, and a member of the Leaders' Meeting and Children's Work Commission. I have served as camp director for our children's camps, counsellor for youth camps and youth leader in the South Caribbean. I have had the opportunity to visit a number of countries through my involvement with the Church, with friends and with Disabled Peoples' International (DPI). These experiences are precious to my development and I look forward to putting into practice the things I learned from these experiences whenever possible.

At the same time, I worked on my chosen vocation, dressmaking. I must say that the success I experience in this field is due to encouragement from my mother, who made available the necessary materials, as well as my own determination to do something with my life. After many attempts, I was able to teach myself to sew. In 1950, after my stay in hospital, I decided to make dressmaking a paying business. I have made everything from bridal gowns to burial gowns. I have also had the opportunity to train some young women who are now good dressmakers. I am very proud of this fact as it helps me with knowledge of my self-worth. I believe that we are all put here on earth for a reason, and the fact that I have helped someone to learn something means that I have played my part in this life. And I know that I have a reason to live. I do not feel that I have been a burden to my family or my community. So far I have mentioned most of the positive aspects of my life, but it has not been all easy sailing. One of the things I have learned in coping with a disability is that if you are positive, you can cope much better. So I find it easier to relate the things that help, rather than the things that hinder.

The two most outstanding negative things in my life are my mobility (or rather, lack of) and my personal relationships. These are the two areas of my life that I have most problems with.

I find personal relationships most difficult to handle as I am a very emotional person. I treat my personal relationships very privately, so that I would not be able to give detailed accounts in my bid to let you know how I am able to cope. I understand that this is one of the most difficult areas for disabled persons.

I like people a lot and friendships of any kind mean a lot to me. From early childhood I was hurt very easily by those I loved because I trusted them totally. However, while I get to know a lot of people, I do not get too close as I am afraid of the hurt. My first encounter with love was frightening. He was a neighbourhood friend of mine—a nice young man—and I was so afraid that I was not good enough for him. He was doing very well in school and I felt inadequate. However, we had a wonderful friendship—I was deeply in love with him—and when he left to go abroad to study, the love affair ended but the friendship still remained.

At that time, I could not deal with sexuality and everything that went with it. My feelings of self-worth had not yet surfaced so I was unable to cope with that kind of relationship. I later discovered that I had the capability to love and what we are as human beings means much more than our physical bodies, and one's acceptance of self goes a long way in helping others to accept us.

I know now that if I could live my life again I would handle my personal relationships a lot differently. By this I mean that I would have had more faith in myself and I would not have let some of the opportunities that I was afraid of, pass by. But I have learned a lot from my encounters with people, so that when a friendship of any kind falls through, I do not blame it on my disability. I no longer think that I am not good enough—maybe not suited, but never not good enough.

My latest involvement is with DPI, a self-help organization of disabled people, where I am now working with persons with different disabilities. I find this new area of work very challenging as I am discovering new types of disabilities and also finding out how little the general public knows about disability and disabled persons. I therefore feel we, as disabled people, have an important role to play in this process of educating the population. Disabled persons will always be with us and the need for others to understand us, and our need to be understood, is real.

My involvement with DPI is helping me to continue my progress towards self-worth. I know that I have a lot to learn from my disabled brothers and sisters, as well as my able-bodied friends, for we must not isolate ourselves. Where there is a will there is a way. Let's find that way.

SUPPORT, SUCCESS, STRUGGLE

Eunice Fiorito
with Jim Doherty
UNITED STATES

AS A CHILD, I was a tomboy—playing at street hockey and bicycle races, climbing trees and falling out of them, learning to win and lose in competition with the boys. Some say that, as an adult, I continue to be a tomboy, competing with men for leadership positions and not accepting traditional women's roles.

My parents always supported my active, aggressive lifestyle, both before and after I became blind. I never once heard the phrase, "Be a lady!" I have always been grateful to my mother and father for helping me to develop an assertive personality, self-confidence, and a belief that anything I wanted to do was, in fact, possible.

I took my love of competition into the classroom and school activities. My principal extra-curricular interests in high school and as a young adult were music and theatre. Losing my sight at age sixteen only temporarily interrupted my enjoyment of and participation in these activities. I later drew on that training in meeting professional challenges.

Throughout my career, I have felt discrimination more often on the basis of sex than because of my disability. Ironically, the one time I felt most strongly that disability was the issue, other women were the discriminators.

My first encounter with anti-female prejudice came soon after I completed my undergraduate degree. I had taken a special course of training to prepare myself to be a rehabilitation teacher, and scored a ninety-nine percent on the state civil service examination in Illinois. Three men had also taken the course, and when a position came open in Chicago—in the very field for which I had been trained—one of them was appointed, even though he had scored lower than I on the examination. To me, this was obvious sex discrimination, and I said so in no uncertain terms. With the help of a family friend on the governor's staff, I took my complaint to the highest officials in the state and got the job.

At this point I should say that, in my early working years, I was blessed with excellent supervisors. My first was a black man who was not only comfortable working with a blind woman but was also supportive and helpful. He suggested that I not limit myself to the opportunities possible with just an undergraduate degree. I took that advice and went on to obtain a master's degree in social work. My first job after graduate school was at the Jewish Guild for the Blind in New York. If I had been asked to design the perfect environment for a fledgling social worker, this would have been it. I was able to develop my skills and professionalism in a very pleasant atmosphere, both on and off the job. The only dark spot in the picture was the paternalism of some of the men who ran various programs in the agency.

My supervisor this time was a woman who was very sure of herself and her position. When she saw that I exhibited similar qualities, she became a friend and mentor. She taught me how to show others what I was doing and why I was doing it without either boasting or arrogance. I found that this kind of job performance was welcomed by co-workers and superiors. As I progressed to positions of increasing responsibility, I acquired a reputation as a person who got things done.

When New York's Mayor decided to create an office of the handicapped in his administration, I was chosen to be director of that office. The mission of the new agency was to open the economic, social and cultural life of the city to all persons with disabilities. To that end, I met continually with the heads of service agencies, employers' organizations, property managers, landlords and representatives of the entertainment industry, seeking to break down physical and attitudinal barriers that restricted the lives of New York's disabled residents and visitors. The discrimination I sensed in this position was expressed passively, yet it was still demeaning. The men seemed to look on me as if to say, "Isn't it wonderful that this blind lady can do such a good job." But they did not seem to doubt my ability to do the job. My position as director of an office whose primary concern was expanding opportunities for disabled New Yorkers brought with it a great deal of visibility. It also brought the respect that usually accrues to anyone with the title "director." Therefore, anyone who might have been prejudiced toward me, either as a woman or as a disabled person, could not display that feeling with total impunity.

In 1976, I experienced the most blatant discrimination I had yet encountered. Women throughout the nation and from all walks of life were laying the groundwork for a national conference on women's issues to be held in Houston, Texas in 1977. Disabled women were totally excluded from the planning and delegate selection process. Through Bella Abzug, an outspoken former member of the United States Congress and one of the driving forces behind the conference, we arranged for nine of us to attend the meetings as "observers." When we arrived, we discovered that a position paper on the concerns of disabled women had already been written—with no input whatsoever from any disabled women. With the help of the lesbian delegates—another group whose members do not fit into any convenient minority cubicle—we succeeded in forcing rejection of the original paper and adoption of one we wrote ourselves. Regrettably, and probably unconsciously, the women at the conference had adopted society's habit of doing *for* disabled people, rather than working *with* us or letting us handle our own affairs. Some at least, I have found, learned a valuable lesson from that experience.

Partly as a result of some contacts I made during the women's conference, I moved from New York to my present position in Washington, DC, as Special Assistant to the Commissioner of the Rehabilitation Services Administration in the Department of Education. The move to Washington brought many changes, professional as well as personal. In New York, I had been the decision-maker, the Director. In my new position, I was to have input into the decisions, but not the final say. That adjustment was comparatively easy for me to make. More difficult to cope with was the reception I got from my new colleagues, most of whom were men.

I soon learned that, in spite of all the advances women have made, men in Washington do not yet automatically accept us as equally capable co-workers, particularly if, as in my case, the woman is appointed to a position at or above the men's level of responsibility. I think I can risk generalization and say that in Washington we have the ultimate crystalization of gender-based discrimination. Men must tolerate women in the professions because the law says they must, but they do not have to treat us as equals. To advance in her field, a woman must prove herself every step of the way, while men are not held to such rigid standards. Men expect other men to be capable and to succeed, so they move each other along career ladders with or without the necessary qualifications. For example, if and when a woman is promoted to a senior level within government, she is first placed in an "acting" position to test her competence and potential. Men, however, are promoted without a similar testing or proving period.

We *are* making some progress, largely because the women's movement continues to struggle for equality. Disabled people should adopt that same determination.

From 1973 to 1977, we joined forces and fought vigorously to make our government implement Section 504 through its regulations. When that job was completed, the energy, unity and purpose which we had just dissipated. Section 504 only prohibited discrimination against persons with disabilities by organizations that received federal grants for contracts.

In 1985 a new fight began to broaden the rights of disabled people who were not covered under Section 504. After a five-year struggle, in August 1990 the Americans with Disabilities Act became law. The regulations for its implementation have been taking effect over the past year. Now that this goal has been achieved, the fire again appears to be going out of our movement.

Taking ADA as our Civil Rights Act should be as challenging and exciting as were our earlier battles. Making it work, initiating complaints, working with community groups, employers, public facilities, etc., and, if necessary, entering into class action procedures, are activities that all of us should be involved in, to secure our rights as women and citizens.

A review of my professional life would not be complete without prominent mention of the role models with whom I have been lucky enough to share some part of that life. These disabled women not only supported me when times got tough, they also, with their advice and by their example, often corrected my thinking and pointed me in the proper direction. I hope all of us who have achieved some manner of success will stand ready to do the same for other disabled women who are still searching for a productive place in society.

To sum up: my career and my successes were made possible by early support from my parents, a good foundation of training and education, a bit of luck along the way, excellent disabled female role models and my own attitude that tells the world, "I am here! I am capable! I will succeed!"

To disabled women just entering the world of work or seeking to better their positions, I would say: go confidently with determination into whatever arena or daily competition you have chosen. Know yourselves and your abilities; do not hide, either, from the scrutiny of others. And when, as so often happens, the challenges grow beyond anticipated dimensions, come to us, your sisters. We will accept you and support you, praise and correct you and assist you in returning to the struggle renewed and ready for new strivings, new successes.

BATTLING WITH ADVERSITY

Zhang Li
PEOPLE'S REPUBLIC OF CHINA

COMING INTO THE WORLD

There is a well-known remark, "The deeper the suffering is, the greater the possibility of success will be!"

I was a prematurely-delivered baby in Beijing and spent my first months in an incubator. Then, I was carried home by my parents. But my young mother, looking at me—the sick baby—was at her wits end. In tears, she thought aloud, "How can I bring this baby up?"

Grandmother, who had come to see us at that moment, took me to her home. Upon entering the house, Grandfather roared at the sight of me: "You have brought such a sick baby home! Can we raise her? Oh! How could we bear to let our daughter down if something terrible happens?"

Watching me silently, Grandmother said nothing.

My arrival not only broke the tranquility at Grandmother's, making endless trouble for her, it caused more sighs in the family. In spite of the fact that I tided over the dangerous period in the incubator, I was still very weak and could not be compared with any other babies.

Other babies my age could be breastfed, but I could not. With difficulties, Grandmother had to nurse me drop by drop with a small spoon several times every day. She spent such a long time doing this that her back would ache, but she would never complain. She would stay up to look after me until the small hours, while everyone else had fallen into a sound sleep. In this way, Grandmother spent many sleepless nights, and at the same time greeted countless golden daybreaks.

A year dragged out. Grandmother's efforts were not in vain. I survived, growing bigger, gaining more weight, and my pale face became rosy! I became a lovely child! The frowns could no longer be seen and the sighs of Grandfather could not be heard, either. He got to love me. Every evening after work, the first thing he would do was take me in his arms and kiss me. He would say, "What a lovely child! Don't you miss Grandfather?" With these words, he would hold me up high above his head!

But I still could not sit up at the age of three or four, and I was unable to move my legs and arms. Besides, my whole body was constantly twisting. Again, dark clouds covered the family and my parents sighed from time to time. They began to take me to hospitals to ask for help. Each time they went with hope but returned in disappointment. The doctors would always shake their heads, saying, "The child has got cerebral palsy. It is a difficult disorder. Up to now, it is incurable."

At the age of three or four, I was learning about the world earlier than others of my age. I gradually became aware of the fact that I was not the same as other children around me. I was lying in bed all day long, and I could neither stand nor sit up. I was living a separate existence from the outside world.

It was time to go to school at the age of seven. The children nearby entered school, one by one. I felt worried and upset at the happy looks on their faces. I could still remember the day when my little friend, Qingqing, came to my home with a new school-bag on her shoulder. She cried out happily while she was still outside my room, "LiLi, I am going to school tomorrow. Look! My Mom has bought me a schoolbag!" Looking at her, I was even more disturbed. How wonderful it would be if I could be with them too! Thinking of reality, I cried, and asked Grandmother to let me go to school. Grandmother, of course, was at a loss as to what to do and could only let me make a tearful scene at my convenience in her arms.

The unforgettable year of 1966 witnessed days filled with tears and misfortune. The storm of "The Cultural Revolution" raided Grandmother's home from the very beginning. Grandfather was persecuted (denounced and paraded through the streets) and even Grandmother was sent back to her hometown to be "re-educated" by poor peasants. Their tribulation caused me to part from them, crying and shouting. Where could I go after leaving them?

Dad, being a so-called capitalist-roader, was forced to work and at home only Mom was with the kids. She was really unable to support the three of us. In such circumstances, I came to the Welfare Institution in early June 1966.

STUDYING WITH THE BEST OF CARE IN THE MOTHERLAND

Being away from my dear grandparents, parents and other family members, I felt badly upset and my childish heart was greatly harmed. I cried hopelessly, although crying was of no use. Then merciless reality took me into an entirely new world.

I was sincerely welcomed by all in the institution. Uncles, aunts and little friends not only greeted me with open arms, but showed their deep love for me as well. At mealtime, when the wardmates were enjoying their dishes, I had no appetite at all. I turned my face aside, shedding tears. Then, aunts there would come to my bed to spoonfeed me, saying, "LiLi, do not cry, we love you just like your Grandmother."

Little wardmates also came to comfort me, "No crying please, OK? We will tell you stories. Is that alright?" They took turns reading picture books to me and it was their stories that quieted me. Even now, interesting stories still remain fresh in my mind, too wonderful to be forgotten.

A few years' time flew quickly and soon I was fourteen years of age. My increasing age made me think, "All my friends can read and write while I know nothing. If only I could do the same." Little by little, a strong desire rooted itself in my heart. I would learn to read and write.

I saved the pocket money Mom gave me and asked others to buy me pencils and notebooks. You can never imagine how happy I was when I saw these pencils and notebooks.

Immediately I began to work. Unfortunately, my hands were continuously twisting. How could I pick up the pencil? Even if I was able, with difficulties, to pick it up, the pencil would slip from my hand before I could finish writing a single word.

After several days' practice, I met with failure. One after another, the pencils were broken and not one word was written out. I cried in distress at the twisting hands. Was it true that I would never write? I was vexed and did some hard thinking. Finally, the strong desire for learning won. To my great pleasure, I found out that I could hold the pencil in my mouth. I remembered that when I was a little child, my friends would play building blocks with their hands and the little blocks were turned into a large building. I had been eager to join them, yet my hands were useless. What could be done? In my urgency, I had used my mouth. So, I was sure I could use my mouth to write, too.

Holding the pencil in my mouth, I tried hard to write. When the tip of a pencil was broken, wardmates would sharpen it for me so that I could continue practising. At last I could write, although the words were hardly presentable. Normal people cannot understand the hardship I have gone through.

The first difficulty I met with was the shortness of the distance between my eyes and the paper. Scarcely had I finished a word when I became dizzy and felt like vomiting. It's really unthinkable how I endured it, but I didn't give up.

Day and night, during unbearable hot midsummer evenings, while the rest all went out to enjoy the cool in their wheelchairs, I was at my wheelchair writing. Beads of sweat fell from my forehead onto the notebook. My shirt was soaked through. I passed the nights under the reading lamp, with a notebook and a short pencil.

A year later I finally succeeded! How happy I was after finishing my first diary in recognizable handwriting!

MY WORKS BEING PUBLISHED

"You are a severely handicapped person. What causes you to continue the struggle and pursue a lofty ideal?" Whenever I was asked this question by friends, I would answer without the slightest hesitation, "Books." Reading has given me courage as well as strength. Boundless knowledge has helped me to overcome the agony of serious disability and wiped away grievous tears at the same time.

I will never forget the day when my first poem was published. No words could express my feelings. It was several years ago. One day, a wardmate came happily to my bed and asked, mysteriously, holding a newspaper in her hand, "LiLi, could you guess what a piece of good news I've brought for you?"

I shook my head, "Oh! What's the good news?"

"Your poem is published!" She waved the paper at me.

"What?" I didn't take it to heart. "Don't kid me! I don't believe it."

So she showed the article to me. Sure! Hardly believing it, I saw with my own eager eyes: *Song of Spring—by Zhang Li, the handicapped.* "My work has turned into type and my dreams have come true!" Tears were running down my cheek ...

Why? I had endured hardships, the torment of the disability, and shed many tears in disappointment. Through hard work, I had made progress rapidly at the beginning of my self-study. I was able to read newspapers and novels, and write diaries in about a year's time. I could even write to Grandmother. So wonderful was the result that I kept on reading, reading, day and night. Books have become my inseparable friends.

The first novel I read was *How the Steel is Tempered!* The image of Baoer impresses me deeply. Then, I thought of myself and thought of his saying that life comes to us only once and we should make the best use of it. We should not regret idleness, nor feel ashamed of being common and inactive.

Baoer, the hero in the novel, even though paralyzed in bed and blind in both eyes, used his pen as a weapon, bravely fighting with merciless fate. Compared to him, I'm luckier, because I've got a pair of bright eyes.

Why weren't you writing earlier, one may wonder. It was a bit too difficult for me because I had no schooling at all. But I persisted in it. Indescribable happiness was with me when I finished the first poem. I mailed it immediately to a certain magazine office. Then, I waited. A day, a week, a month ... Finally, in a few months, my manuscript was sent back. "A failure is nothing to me," I said to myself. "If I go with it, I'm sure to succeed!" Yet the fact is, it was not as simple as I thought it would be.

From then on, I sent my manuscripts to various newspaper offices and publishing houses, waiting for the day when my works would be published. Nevertheless, I got them back dozens of times in a row. Looking at the papers piled up on the desk, I sighed painfully, tears dripping down on them.

Then, I really felt disheartened and I laughed at myself: "Without any schooling, you want to engage in writing?" I tore the papers I was writing to pieces and threw away my pen. Again,

I was in a deep depression. Knowing about this, my friends wrote to me. Some told me of their own experiences, and comforted and encouraged me to persist in writing and self-learning. They also sent me books to help me learn more about the fundamentals of writing, and they urged me not to shrink back from difficulties. All this help moved me to enthusiasm and heightened my confidence. I tried again. Countless nights passed. I could not remember the number of pens broken and the times when my lips were grazed by pens. Later, after I sent them my published poems, friends shared my happiness, saying, "You've finally succeeded, LiLi."

In recent years, some of my works have been published at home and abroad. In 1987, an autobiographical prose piece of mine was published in *The Rehabilitation Gazette* in the United States. The works were praised by friends in and out of the country and my spirit of painstaking self-learning moved handicapped people in particular.

With the publication of my works, I've received numerous letters brimming with warm feelings. I'm deeply touched, too. A girl who had one hand deformed in an accident wrote to me, "Dear sister, I thought myself to be the most unfortunate one in the world. Life was cruel to me because I've lost one of my dear hands. I cried and sighed over it. Just at the time when I wanted to end life, I read about your achievements. I will live like you ..." More wrote to ask me to be their friends. A middle school pupil said, "Dear LiLi, I'd like you to be my elder sister. If you agree, I'd be the happiest one in the world!" Apart from this, friends sent me love letters, proposing to be my lifelong companion.

I was moved to tears. Having the best of care by people around me, I, a severely handicapped person, felt very happy, living in a warm society. Besides, I've come to realize the value of my existence. Disabled as I am, I'm not good-for-nothing. I've got a lofty ideal and I still strive to reach it.

At the moment, in addition to writing, I've been learning English from the TV. After two years, I'm now able to read letters by friends from abroad with the aid of the dictionary, and I can also have simple conversations. Translation is still difficult for me. And finally, I firmly believe that in the near future, holding the pen in my mouth, I'm sure to make greater progress and write out more beautiful poems in Chinese!

THE PATH

A winding path
In front of me,
Stretches to the horizon
In walking along the path again
At this moment,
On and on,
leaving my deep footprints.

My path,
long and meandering
I've known all about you,
The tall straight poplars,
The vigorous weeds along the path,
And all those innumerable small stones.
Engraved on my mind,
They could never be forgotten.

Oh, my familiar path,
Wandering along you every day,
You will remember all my failures and sighs,
All my secrets and delights,
Watered by my pain
Invigorated by my joy,
Just like my sweetheart.

Now spring is awakening,
Sprouting willows stroking my face,
Returning swallows singing before my eyes,
Spring breeze, spring sunlight,
Spring in the air,
Spring along my path.

— Zhang Li

Dance

zana
UNITED STATES

MY LIFE STORY

Mikiko Misono
JAPAN

MY NAME IS MIKIKO MISONO. I am a quadraplegic because of an injury to my cervical vertebrae, C3 and C4. I am also hard of hearing. On top of that, I have a blood disease. I got these handicaps four years ago. At that time I was a student at a nursing school, but after my injury, I was not eligible to study at the nursing school anymore. I spent six months in a hospital, then I rented an apartment in Tokyo. I wanted to go back to Fukuoka, which is where I am from. But my father had cancer then, and my mother had just had a heart operation, so they were not able to take care of me. I decided to live by myself in Tokyo.

Every day I went out looking for a job. But at that time, I still had not been approved as a legally handicapped person, so I did not have a handicapped person's handbook. For this reason, no employer would hire me. I earned money for living expenses by gathering empty cans and scrap iron which had been thrown into the streets. I also collected old newspapers to sell.

Of course, we have a Daily Life Security Law in Japan, but in order to get approved, we must fill out many application forms which have many items. Furthermore, we have to submit each application form to respective offices. It is not so difficult for those who understand the legal system. Even though I had studied something of our legal system during my time at the nursing school, I didn't understand the welfare system in detail. The amount of the pension for which I was eligible at that time was much lower than that which other handicapped people were receiving. Though I really tried hard to find a job, none was offered to me and my cost of living was much higher now than when I had been living in the hospital. So, I decided to go to the Ministry of Welfare to study the Daily Life Security Law.

The man I met at the office was very kind and taught me how

to fill out the forms. After submitting these forms, I was able to receive about the same amount of pension as other handicapped people did. However, I still could not get any job at all. I consulted a caseworker and told him that I wanted to go to a university or a vocational school to study. He told me that anyone on a Social Security pension is not allowed to attend school. Feeling very disappointed, I again began to gather empty cans and sometimes I held bazaars to earn money.

One day I met a man who understood me well. I became his home helper. He is also a quadraplegic, due to a injury to his cervical vertebra. I used to go to his house at about the time he came home from work. I cooked for him and ate dinner with him at his home. I took his laundry back to my house, washed it and took it back to him the following day. I worked this way for about one year, even on rainy days and snowy days. Sometimes it took me two hours to come and go in my wheelchair. One time, when I left his home about midnight, I made a joke: "It's always Cinderella time!"

No private enterprises offer a job to a person with multiple handicaps like me. And without a college degree, it was impossible for me to get a job related to mass communication. I was very shocked when I was even refused admission at a vocational centre for handicapped persons. They said, "You don't have to work. You can get a pension." In such a circumstance, I felt very happy when a man, who also had a handicap like mine, took a special interest in me. The greatest pleasure I have now is that he has become my husband.

My husband is a civil servant and his salary is not so high. So I tried to think of what I could do. There were several handicapped women around me who were also refused education and employment for various reasons. I asked them to get together and start a class where we could learn to become instructors of flower arrangement. At the same time, we started to offer some English classes for fatherless children. We are currently deriving a lot of satisfaction from these activities.

These days, we, as members of this handicapped group, keep in contact and help each other. For instance, we ask visually handicapped people to come to our houses and clean the rooms. Sometimes we ask physically handicapped people who can drive to take us somewhere in their cars. When we ask the help of those who are hard of hearing, we communicate by writing notes back and forth on paper. In this way, we can communicate, and we are very grateful to them for their help. We are all handicapped, but we live our independent lives by extending helping hands to each other. Our group is still very small, but its name is big: the Committee for the Promotion of Individual Autonomy. Whenever we need help, we call on each other and help each other. So we call ourselves "care helpers."

Today in Japan, the Equal Employment Opportunity Law has been enacted. But the percentage of handicapped women who have jobs is still very low. Of course, multiply-handicapped women have even less of an opportunity. I have tried to figure out why this is the case, and I have found out that this law is not clear as to how many handicapped women should be hired, or how many multiply-handicapped women should be hired.

There may seem to be many problems to solve, but I think they can be solved if we each keep in mind our individual importance as human beings—as worthwhile and useful human beings—no matter how severe our handicaps may be. It is important to strive for better communication with people around us and in society at large so that opportunities for us to work will appear.

In closing, let me say that I am praying that everyone who hopes to meet a wonderful partner, as I have met my husband, will do so. And if you do, please let us know so that we can send you a congratulatory telegram!

SHADOWS OF THE PAST

Ventura Emma
ITALY

SHADOWS ON SHADOWS in front of my eyes, fighting a duel to make one stand on top of the other. All of them make me feel uneasy and anxious. The shadows of the night enshroud me in their black and stuffy cloak, rousing fear in me. The shadows of the past take me back in time, revealing without any pity my frustrated feelings and that part of the past which has conditioned all my life. Denuded of that discretion which for years concealed my sentiments to unknown eyes, I subject myself to an unconditional surrender, as if I am in a movie sequence.

Five years old, a train running fast on the rails and my mother's sad look. Scoliosis, they told me my illness was called. It was an illness that had to be wiped out and for this reason I had to be hospitalized. I would be small and hunch-backed for the rest of my life, and all my movements would be limited. Luckily I did not have to use a wheelchair or crutches and I felt strong, able to face every difficulty that I was to meet. But at that time, in my childish heart, I could not know that my strength was just an illusion.

During the journey I remained with my nose pressed to the window all the time. I had never been on a train and those trees, those houses which seemed to come towards me, gave me a feeling of rapture and excitement. It did not take much to make me happy when I was a happy-go-lucky child. I still did not know that, in a short time, a too precocious maturity would bury the thoughtlessness of childhood. When we arrived at the station I looked around, astonished. I compared that big station with our small one. Everything was new to me except the warm hug of my aunt who came and fetched us to her home. I was fond of her, as if she was a second mother. The idea of seeing her house for the first time excited me. The day soon passed in playing with my cousins and running about the town.

The next day I felt bewildered and agitated while I was sitting with my mother in the waiting room of the hospital. There was no longer a trace of the fun and the happiness of the previous day. I had a lump in my throat and the thousand questions that I wanted to ask my mother remained buried in my mind. I was not able to say a word.

Then everything happened as if I were in a trance: my mother kissed me whispering something that I did not grasp and then went away. When I saw her departing along the corridor, I shook off my torpor and cried and cried at the top of my voice. I could feel someone holding me back with all his force, preventing me from running after her—someone who I considered to be an enemy because he was separating me from my mother. I found myself free in the moment that my mother was vanishing from my sight, and a door shut inexorably behind her. When the evening came, I was seized with fear. I sobbed for my mother, even though I thought I had no more tears to shed. Nobody gave me any comfort, nobody understood what I was feeling.

Then the night came, and someone switched the light off, leaving me completely in the dark. That shrouded darkness frightened me. I hid myself in the bed, trembling like a leaf in the wind. Everything was unknown and hostile around me. Scared to death, with wide-open eyes fixed in the darkness, which for me concealed a thousand dangers, I counted every minute and every hour of the night. Only at daybreak did my eyelids become heavier and heavier and finally I fell asleep.

Children should never be separated from their parents for any reason in the world; there is no good reason for it. I remember that I withdrew with my mother when she came to visit me because I did not want to share the joy of being together with her with anyone else. We talked and she told me that she would come to see me every day—it was a promise. Reluctantly, I accepted the idea that in a few minutes she would go away again. I was growing up and, strangely, that knowledge did not give me any comfort. For two long months, days passed inexorably slowly and I lived only for those meetings with my mother.

Finally, they imprisoned my chest in a coat of plaster, which suffocated me, but I learned to accept it because my mother had explained that it was to make me better, and I wanted that with all my might. I was sure that I would be normal again, so I accepted that I had to wear the plaster, even if it prevented me from making any movements. My mother also told me that she would take me back home in a few days. I was longing to see my house again, to hug my father and my brothers. A few days later, I went on a train which took me back home to my safe and comfortable refuge. I wore that plaster for forty days and then my mother told me that I had to go back to the hospital to take it off. They took off the plaster, but there had not been any improvement in my condition. Thus, my suffering began again.

I returned to my loved ones, but, for me, nothing was the same. I had changed. I no longer had my childish heart but an adult one. I was well aware of my state and of the difficulties that I would meet in life. Two very long months in hospital had been useless. They only increased the terror of the dark in me and had given me a premature maturity.

I remember my first day at school and how I stood aside because I knew I was different from the other girls, who looked at me with curiosity. Their looks were innocent, but what sufferings they caused! I also remember the day my teacher exposed me to my companions' eyes, like an animal in an exhibition. She clearly explained my physical deformities, underlining the word "poor" before my name. That word caused me great grief, more than my companions' looks. Nobody understood that I wished to be accepted, not to be pitied. I did not want to see those compassionate looks of pity that made my physical diversity seem more burdensome. Every look directed towards my body was like a razor blade that slowly and relentlessly injured my spirit. It was in these moments that I felt my desperation grow immeasurably, until it made my heart burst. I wanted to be considered just like any other normal living person on the face of the earth, with normal hopes and feelings and the courage to face up to life, whatever it had in store for me. This was the only thing my eyes implored to the people who surrounded me.

Later, my school companions accepted me and learned to love me. I began to have more security within the classroom; but outside everything was different. The comments on my physical appearance and peoples' pitiful looks affected me deeply. Sometimes I felt a great need to cry but I smothered it with my strength of pride. I was perfectly aware of the fact that my life would always be alternating between bitterness and sufferings, just as I was aware of all those things that I was going to have to renounce once I became an adult. I knew for sure that I would have to renounce forming a family of my own and the satisfaction of my senses, suffocating even the smallest physical desire. I knew that I would always be "left aside" from a sexual point of view. I would never be able to receive those privileges that society had reserved only for "normal" people. To the harassing question of whether this was fair or not, I have always answered, no, it certainly was not, in my point of view. But I was on the other side of the barricade.

And what about the point of view of others? I realized that I could never condemn a person who could not have a sexual relationship with a disabled person. The things that we find right are like a breath of wind, that we desperately try to imprison in our grip. On the other hand, after all, perhaps nature had been a little generous with me because it had given me a high intelligence.

I did well in my studies and this has been my only source of satisfaction. I had also received another gift in life: my sensitivity, which, although it caused me a great deal of suffering, seemed to continue to develop for this very reason. This sensitivity has taught me to love animals, which are considered with contempt by most people. This sensitivity allows me to understand that they are also living beings, suffering from being misunderstood, suffering injustices, and they have as much right to live as human beings have.

Many years have passed since then, and now I am an adult, but even if my maturity has been too premature, I do not feel inwardly old. There is one hope hidden in my heart. I have been indulging in it for very many years. It is the passport to my solitude, the satisfaction of my senses. I cannot exactly explain what it is that pushes me to write, that has led my hand and my mind, but it is beyond my control. I could see that I was gradually being absorbed into my world, which was full of fantasy, and I was becoming part of it. I soon realized that it was impossible for me to keep away from this world and even if I had wished to do so, my willpower was completely overcome by this tremendous passion for writing. I felt that I had to give birth to my fantasy, isolating myself from the rest of the world, and in this way, I finally felt myself a complete woman. All the bitterness and suffering, solitude and regrets seemed to melt away. I found myself in a timeless and new dimension.

I could see that writing for me had become a vital force without which I would have declared the death of inner spirit. I have struggled strongly to make a name for myself in the literary world, but, at the beginning, I received only bitter and painful disappointments, so I decided to give it all up. For years, I denied what I deeply believed in, but I consoled myself with my poetry. Then, all at once, this violent passion for narrative writing started to burn in my heart again, asking me how on earth I could have resisted all this time. I felt as if I had denied my child.

The narrative is a passion risen from my heart, a passion which has put a gleam of light in the far depths of my soul, a tiny spark in the middle of the gloomy darkness of my life. It is a passion which allows me to isolate myself from the rest of the world if I choose. However, this will only happen when I am able to accomplish my aspirations and thus feel fulfilled. And finally, in the eyes of the world I will not only be a body to look at, but a person to remember.

IV

IN SPITE OF THE WORLD

It was a woman who, like me, has a spinal curvature so the two sides of her body don't match. She had decided to wear a bikini, and her statement to the world was: "I am Raquel Welch as seen through the eyes of Picasso."

— Rebecca Burns *United States*
  (Yvonne Duffy, *...All Things are Possible*, Ann Arbor, Michigan: A.J. Garvin and Associates, 1981, p. 51.)

Sexuality is much more than the sexual act. The biggest sexual organ is the brain.

— Irene Feika *Canada*
  ("Sexuality Presentation," at the Women in Development Leadership Training Seminar, Roseau, Dominica, July 1988, sponsored by Disabled Peoples' International.)

IN A WORLD WHICH has a narrow definition of beauty and then upholds the "body beautiful," most women don't measure up. Women with disabilities continue to grapple with the meaning of society's definition for their bodies. In this section, they decide that difference, variation, is beautiful, and every woman is beautiful. Furthermore, they confirm that the ability or desire to have sex does not depend upon how much one's body conforms to social definitions of beauty. We are all human, and therefore sexual. These writers proclaim that we are, in spite of the world, *women*.

Elizabeth Semkiw of Canada offers a gallery of women,

proclaiming her vision of womankind. Theresia Degener discusses how women with disabilities in Germany have been sterilized involuntarily by parents and institutions, and how the sexuality of disabled people has been denied.

In Nigeria, explains Ntiense Ben Edemikpong, the practice of female genital mutilation denies women's sexuality and disables them mentally and physically. The Women's Centre in Nigeria has organized against this practice through public awareness campaigns in the countryside and the media.

Lesley Hall writes about how Australian women with disabilities are fighting back against cultural attitudes about women's bodies. In Australia, beauty quests or pageants are often used to raise money for disabled people's programs. The Women with Disabilities Feminist Collective has been leading a campaign calling for the abolition of such quests.

Finally, Amber Coverdale Sumrall of the United States embarks on a backpacking trip and discusses the impact of the trip on her body image of herself as a woman with a disability. She proclaims her acceptance of her body's limitations and, most of all, its strength.

THE REVELATION OF HUMAN EXPERIENCE

Elizabeth Semkiw
CANADA

Manuel

Centred

The Face of Struggle

THE REVELATION OF HUMAN EXPERIENCE

CONTINUED

Silent One

A Time for Sadness

Coming to Terms

Too Much, Too Soon

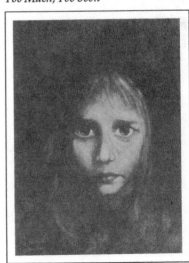

STERILE WITHOUT CONSENT

Theresia Degener
GERMANY

IN 1984, THE WEST GERMAN media started to pay attention to the issue of sterilization. This was partly due to the discovery by historians that many of the girls in schools for the mentally disabled had been sterilized without their consent or against their will. After these findings were publicized, a television program "Panorama" was devoted to this topic. On "Panorama," a mother explained that she had had her disabled daughter sterilized at the request of her daughter's teacher. The teacher requested sterilization because the children were going on an overnight field trip and he did not want to be responsible in the event that the girl engaged in sexual activity and became pregnant.

In fact, many institutions in West Germany require the sterilization of mentally handicapped girls as a prerequisite for admittance. The institutions don't want to deal with the possibility of a pregnant disabled woman. Parents of disabled teenagers are often intimidated by the sexuality of their children and are fearful of a potential pregnancy.

"Panorama" alerted the public to these issues—many Social Democrats and much of the alternative press were horrified at these findings. Many who protest this abuse of sterilization draw parallels between the current situation and the forced sterilization that occurred under the Nazis. An estimated 400,000 people were sterilized against their will or without their consent during the Nazi era. Currently, there is a heated debate about whether or not the federal government should provide compensation for those who underwent forced sterilization.

The present West German criminal code clearly states that sterilization is illegal unless it is performed with the consent of the affected and if this consent is not against ethical principles. Sterilization against a person's will or without her consent is only permissible if there is a present danger to the health of that person. However, some people claim that there is a gap in the law, in that it does not say anything about those who are mentally unable to give consent themselves. Some intermediate courts have ruled that the consent of the disabled person can be replaced by the consent of the parent or legal representative in cases where the disabled person is incapable of making her own decision. This is not legal, however, as the law does not allow for this option. The legal system in West Germany is not a case system like the United States where the rule of precedence must be followed. Courts in West Germany do not look to precedents set by other courts, but rather they must find the answer in the law itself.

Lebenshilfe, the largest organization for the parents of disabled persons, is one of the main proponents of involuntary sterilization. It was founded in the 1950s and it runs "sheltered workshops"—places where disabled people are employed. It runs several other institutions and even has its own publishing house. *Lebenshilfe* and many other parents not organized through *Lebenshilfe* want a new law legalizing the sterilization of mentally disabled people because they don't want their children to become pregnant. Many of the parents feel that because they have already exerted so much energy raising a disabled child, they don't want the burden of raising their children's children. They claim that sterilization is in the best interest of the children and that there is no place within the institutions that could accommodate a pregnant mentally disabled woman. The common morality on this subject is that mentally disabled persons do not have a right to reproduction.

In the 1960s and 1970s, not much was known about how many people were affected by this practice of sterilization, but recently teachers in Hamburg have revealed that about thirty percent of the girls in special schools for mentally disabled children have been sterilized. These girls are less than eighteen years old—most of them are less than fourteen. It has been easy for parents to have their kids sterilized; doctors agree readily. On the other hand, for able-bodied women, it is very difficult to get a sterilization. If they are under eighteen, it is illegal.

The federal government started an investigation to find out how the federal states and institutions are dealing with the problem.

A special board was created to work out a statute which allows for sterilization without consent. Special education experts say also that what has been done in the past should be made legal.

One major concern parents and institutions have is rape. Many mentally disabled women are raped in institutions, by relatives and in the streets. However, there are no available statistics on the subject. Mentally disabled women are in particular danger because they cannot communicate the same way we communicate; they can be easy victims. Proponents of sterilization claim that they want to prevent the repercussions of rape, namely conception, since many of them are Catholic and cannot agree with abortion. I think it is very cynical to deal with the problem of rape by sterilizing disabled women.

Eugenics is another concern. There is a big discussion about eugenic thinking and of new developments in the fields of genetic engineering and reproductive technology. Udo Sierck, who is disabled and has done a lot of work on this issue, has discovered that some genetic counselling offices which are provided by the state in West Germany also provide sterilization recommendations for other doctors. The recommendations are most often based on social behaviour. If you are in a special institution, if your father is an alcoholic, if your uncle is unemployed, if your brother is also in a special institution, you are diagnosed with an inherited disability, and sterilization is recommended. The eugenic arguments used by these counselling offices are currently a hot topic in West Germany, because they remind people of the population control the Nazis planned. Some papers were stolen from some of these offices and published, which was very embarrassing for the people working there. They had difficulties saving their jobs and justifying genetic counselling.

There are a few people, such as progressive educators and church organization members, who criticize the current approach. They propose that we look to other countries for examples of possible alternatives. In Denmark, for instance, there is something called "protected marriages"—houses are provided for mentally disabled couples so that they can live together. Special attendants take care of their needs and the needs of their children. The government provides these services—Denmark is more of a welfare state than West Germany. Reports indicate that these programs are highly successful. The main drawback to the development of further programs is the lack of available funding. This is a big issue in West Germany right now as the social welfare law does not explictly allow for funds to be spent in this way. In addition, most of the disabled parents need supplemental assistance, for they earn minimal wages.

Until recently, disabled people in West Germany were discouraged from having sexual relationships. Many books have been published that state that disabled persons should not have the right to be sexual persons. In many institutions, methods were used to distract disabled people from their sexual feelings. Although it is currently said that mentally disabled people have a right be sexual beings, people are now trying to regulate the circumstances under which disabled persons are allowed to have sexual relationships. There are some people who are supportive of the right of disabled people to explore their sexuality. Several organizations offer services to disabled people who request reproductive counselling. They provide advice on sexual problems and planned parenthood, and help parents to educate their children about birth control.

The conservative West German government is trying to pass a new custody law. There is a provision in that law that states that for disabled people who are unable to give consent for sterilization, the parents or legal representative have the power to approve the procedure. The government wanted to enact this law in September 1987, but was unsuccessful due to the resistance of the Green and Social Democratic parties. These parties are very sensitive to this issue, in part because of their work to get compensation for Nazi sterilization victims. The Greens and Social Democrats are supportive of the reforms in the new custody law, except the provision dealing with the sterilization of disabled people. The government had therefore excluded the controversial provision in order to pass the reform of the custody law. But the government will continue its fight to legalize the involuntary sterilization of disabled persons.

I think that one major problem is that many people believe that the reproductive choices of disabled people are a public issue and not a private right. There is also a prevailing attitude that disability is abnormal and therefore unacceptable. If one examines current developments in the fields of genetic engineering and reproductive technology, one can see that people have little tolerance for abnormalities, diseases and disabilities. I think the motivation behind this intolerance is related to the desire to keep a "superior" gene pool in German society—a desire which has a historical base in eugenic actions taken by the Nazis.

In fact, research indicates that many of the women who were sterilized by Nazi orders led lives that today we would call "feminist." In the special Nazi courts that dealt with forced sterilization, these feminist women were labeled "socially disabled" and therefore candidates for sterilization. It is very frightening to see that involuntary sterilization of women continues in West Germany. But now the issue is being debated with an historical perspective that I hope will motivate people to eliminate the attack on disabled women's reproductive rights.

"WE SHALL NOT FOLD OUR ARMS AND WAIT"

Female Genital Mutilation

Ntiense Ben Edemikpong
NIGERIA

IN AFRICA TODAY WOMEN'S voices are being raised against the female genital mutilation that is still practised on babies, little girls and women. These voices belong to a few women who are prepared to call into question the traditional practices that endanger their lives and health. The number of women affected is unknown, but, without a doubt, the total is in the tens of millions.

HISTORICAL PERSPECTIVE

There are no written historic accounts by Africans on the so-called female circumcision, but archaeologists, through the excavation of graves have found mummies in ancient Egypt and Sudan that were excised. Herodotus, the Roman historian (486-424 BC), found the Egyptians practising male and female circumcision when he visited their country around the middle of the fifth century BC, and he reported on it. Strabo, the famous Greek geographer, also reported finding excision of girls a custom when visiting Egypt in 25 BC. Thus circumcision of both girls and boys came into fashion long before Islam, and was practised in many different areas of Africa. The practise was unknown to the Romans until they conquered Egypt and the Middle East.[1]

The forces which motivate a mother to subject her daughters to such drastic operations are different and bewildering. The reasons given are often sexual, religious, hygienic and sociological. Some African societies believe that since the clitoris is an aggressive organ, the operations may diminish a woman's desire for sex and thus erase prostitution. Adherents of some religions like Christianity are of the opinion that circumcision was one of the commands delivered from God to Abraham, and that there was no clear indication in the case of female circumcision.[2]

In the late sixteenth century Jesuit missionaries first came to Ethiopia and converted the people to Roman Catholicism. They met great resistance when they tried to prohibit the excision operations on girls as "pagan" because they thought it was a Jewish rite. When the men were ready to choose wives, they rejected the Catholic converts, but married girls who had undertaken excision. Thus the Catholic community diminished. The missionaries appealed to the Pope at Rome for help and finally the Roman clergies were made to agree to the operations. Since that time, excision has been practiced by all Catholic converts with the consent of the Pope.[3] Muslim theologians also advocate clitoridectomy. Most Muslim men regard virginity as very important and require their brides to prove it by infibulation before the brideprice (or dowry) is paid. In some African societies, female circumcision accompanies initiation rites—when a woman enters adulthood she must be put in seclusion, fattened and circumsized. In some areas, people believe that a woman who is not excised is not clean and that the clitoris excretes something that makes a woman unclean. Thus in some parts of Egypt an uncircumcized woman is called *"Nigsa"* (unclean).

From the above examples, one can see that the whole practice is based on unfounded deductions, ignorance and superstition. In a survey conducted by our Women's Centre in February 1987 in Kenya, East Africa, one hundred prostitutes were interviewed in Mombasa, Kenya's second biggest city; eighty of them admitted to have been circumcized. Therefore, circumcizing a woman to erase prostitution is untenable, since there are some other factors which might urge women into prostitution.[4] Although the Bible approved of circumcision for all Jewish males, it is completely silent over the circumcision of females. Evidence abounds that Jewish males like Abraham, Isaac, John the Baptist, Jesus and Timothy were circumcized, but there is no mention of any Jewish female being circumcized.

Moreover, the so-called circumcized girl who claims to be clean is not actually clean. There are cases of mutilated women with ruptured vaginas or uteruses which cause incontinence later in life, so that they continually dribble urine and have a bad odour throughout their lifetime. Those who practise female circumcision on the grounds of culture should know that culture is based on the beliefs, values and norms of a society, and is subject to modification with the passage of time. A culture that does not take into consideration the dynamism of society as a result of modern innovation, should be shunned completely. Slavery was a cultural practice of many lands in the world and even the Bible and the Koran supported it, but today it is no longer the people's culture. In Africa, the killing of twins and their mothers was one of our cultural practices but thanks to the white missionaries in Africa, this barbaric practice was put to an end.

HOW IT IS DONE

Female circumcision is a misleading term used in Africa to group all kinds of mutilation together. Circumcision as we know it is the cutting of the prepuce or hood of the clitoris, but in Africa more is practised or performed under this guise. Circumcision in its mildest form affects only a small proportion of African women. Besides circumcision, there is "excision," where both the clitoris and the labia minora are removed. Thirdly, the most cruel practice of all is "infibulation" in which the clitoris, both the labia minora and the labia majora, and the outer folds of the skin bordering the vulva are all removed with a blade, knife or pieces of glass, and the two sides of the vulva are closed by scarification or sewing— closing the vagina except for a small opening created by inserting a splinter of wood, for the elimination of urine and menstrual blood.

Most frequently, the operations are carried out by an old woman of the village known as "*Gedda*" in Somalia, or by traditional birth attendants known as "*Daya*" in Egypt and Sudan. In some parts of Nigeria and Mali, village barbers or women of the blacksmith's caste, with knowledge of the occult, perform the operation. More recently, however, mutilations are also being carried out in hospitals in some urban areas in Mali, Somalia, Sudan and Egypt. Studies in Egypt, Sudan and Somalia have reported excisions and infibulation being done by qualified nurses and doctors, but in small numbers. Female children of one month old are also being excised in hospital in Bamako, the capital of Mali. Except in hospitals, anaesthetics are never used. The age at which the mutilations are carried out vary from a few days old, when performed by the Jewish Falashas in Ethiopia, to about seven years old in Egypt and many countries of central Africa, to adolescence among the Ibo and Ibibio tribes of Nigeria.

Elizabeth Inyang Etuk (a member of our women's collective) tells her story:

I was infibulated at the age of five. I remember every bit of it ... The terrible pain and lying tied up for several weeks. It hurt terribly and I cried and cried. I could not understand why this was done to me. When I was thirteen, my aunts examined me and declared that I was not closed enough. They took me to a traditional midwife who lives a few streets away. When I noticed where they were taking me, I tried to run away but they held me tight and dragged me to the midwife's home. They held me down and covered my mouth so that I could not scream. They cut my genitals again and this time the traditional midwife made sure that I was closed.

In terrible pain, I was carried home. I was tied up and could not move, I could not urinate and my stomach became swollen. I was terribly hot one moment and then shaking with cold. Some few days later the midwife came again. I thought she wanted to operate on me again—I screamed and lost consciousness. I woke up in a private hospital's ward. There were moaning women all around me. I did not know where I was and I was in terrible pain. My legs and my genital area were all swollen. Later I was told by the doctor that a re-infibulation had been performed to cut it open to let the urine and puss pass out so that my swollen stomach could subside. I was terribly weak, and did not care anymore. I wanted to die. Why would my mother do this to me? What had I done to be hurt so terribly?

It is years later now. The doctors told me that I can never have children because of the infection. Therefore, there is no one who will marry me; no one wants a wife who cannot have a child. I used to look at my mother and aunts and ask them: "Why did you do this terrible thing to me?"

PHYSICAL DISABILITIES

Female genital mutilation brings chronic infections of the uterus and vagina. The vagina having become, in the case of infibulation, a semi-sealed organ, sometimes a large foreign body forms in the interior of the vagina as a result of the accumulation of mucous secretions. In some infibulated women, the keloid scar formation on the vulval wound can become so enlarged as to obstruct walking. In such cases, the affected women can walk only with the help of crutches.

Moreover, where the labia majora and labia minora have been removed, the vaginal opening does not give way readily during delivery, because of the scar tissue. This can lead to obstructed labour and if the female continues to push, especially when delivering at home (as many African women used to), very extensive tears of the perineum can occur. This may lead to severe bleeding, as major vessels supplying the vagina can be torn through. The tear can also join the vagina and the rectum, leading to recto-vaginal fistula, where the woman's feces passes through the vagina. Or, the tear may link up the vagina with the bladder or urethra or both, leading to vesice-vaginal fistula, and urine being passed through the vagina. Although there are no statistical figures for those with permanent disability, it is believed that thousands of women are affected. Unfortunately, the incidence of disability does not stop the village women from doing circumcisions. When some girls die, either from hemorrhages or infection, this accident is blamed on fate or on an assumption that certain customs have not been properly observed. It is never the responsibility of the operator.

Women with fistulas become social outcasts within their communities, as they smell very badly. They are likely to end up with ascending infection through the bladder to the kidneys or through the uterus into the fallopian tubes, with the consequence of tubal blockage and sterility. Nse Akpan, a thirty-year-old woman from Ugep, Nigeria, says:

I was infibulated at the age of eight and my vagina was closed by sewing amidst terrible physical pain. At eighteen I was married and became pregnant. At childbirth the scar was split to let the baby out. The tough obliterated vulva had lost its elasticity and the head of the baby was pushed through the perineum (which tears more easily than the infibulation scar during the second stage of the labor). However, the baby I delivered died and since then my vagina has been ruptured, leading to the continual dribbling of urine. Although my husband has married a second wife, the shame and the embarrassments that I have been subjected to are greater than if I had been divorced. I rarely sit down in a public gathering or church service for a long time because my dress would be wet around the buttocks, as if I am having menstruation.

Depending upon the degree of mutilation that is carried out, when fully healed, those who have been circumcized end up with scar tissue around the vaginal opening. This opening is not elastic enough, due to the scar tissue, to accommodate the penis and thus does not give way easily during penetration. This can be painful to the female and can make her fearful of sex throughout her lifetime. In addition, clitoral stimulation evokes female orgasm, just as stimulation of the tip of the male penis evokes male orgasm. The earlier a woman is mutilated, the greater is the damage, since infantile and adolescent masturbation teaches the body and the consciousness proper sexual reaction. There is no surgical technique capable of repairing a clitoridectomy, or restoring erogenous sensitivity of the amputated apparatus. The practice, indeed, has affected African women's view of sex, sexuality and relationships with men. It may be considered as another form of female sexual oppression, which is the manipulation of women's sexuality in order to ensure control, domination and exploitation. In specific terms, it serves to harness women into a secondary, submissive role by giving them a negative concept of themselves.

MENTAL DISABILITIES

It is self-evident that any form of surgical interference in the highly sensitive genital organs constitutes a serious threat to the child, and that the painful operation is a source of major psychological, as well as physical, trauma. There are some cases of girls who became neurotic under the threat of an operation or after the operation, and continued to remain in that condition throughout their lifetime. Rose Udobang, a middle-aged woman from Okom in the Ikom Local Government Area in Nigeria, said:

> My twenty-nine-year-old first-born daughter, Ndese Unwaitok, was quite sane and hearty when I took her to the traditional midwife for circumcision at the age of twelve. I never disclosed to her that she was to be circumcized. When she reached the traditional midwife's house, she was arrested by six powerful women and circumcized while she screamed and fainted. Efforts were made to resuscitate her, and ever since she regained consciousness she has been neurotic and mentally unbalanced. She has now been roaming the streets and begging.

Another woman, Ime Etukudo, from Warife in Akamkpa Local Government Area in Nigeria, and a primary school teacher, said:

> I was persuaded by Mother to get my first daughter circumcized according to the tradition of the society. My daughter was seven years old at the time. One evening I told my daughter that I would take her early the following morning for circumcision. That night my daughter began dreaming of snakes and ghosts and shouted thrice. I immediately came to the conclusion that she was under threat of the operation, and woke her up and comforted her that my plan to circumcise her was waived. Since then she has not been dreaming of such hideous things.

There are references to infibulated women being inert, docile and incapacitated. We do not know what it means to a girl or a woman when her central organ of sensory pleasure is cut off, when her life-giving canal is stitched up amid blood and fear and secrecy, while she is forcibly held down and told if she screams she will cause the death of her mother or bring shame on her family. Indeed, such an operation brings with it a sense of humiliation and betrayal by parents, especially by the mother, and the girl or woman sees herself as servile, passive, self-sacrificing and a devoted servant of the home and family.

It is frequently written by Muslim theologians that the cutting of the tip of the clitoris "does no harm." This statement simply means that the man who makes it regards a woman as a baby-producing machine, rather than as a human being. Would this not interfere with her sexuality? Would this not change her personality? A traditional midwife who was asked about the real reason why genital mutilation continues to be practised in some parts of Africa said, "Because men require it. Some men refuse to marry girls who are not operated on. They regard an infibulated girl as one whose virginity has not been broken." Inyang Edward, a traditional ruler from Mfum, in the countryside of Ikom, Nigeria, said, "The psychological resistance and resiliency of a woman is broken by the ordeal of the operation and by depriving her of one of the mainsprings of life (her sexuality). Thus the operation is necessary to make females gentle, so they obey men."

WHAT WE CAN DO

We, of this Women's Centre, strongly condemn this outrageous act and have frequently appealed to many African governments to legislate against this dehumanizing tradition. But legislation alone is not the only weapon, for it may simply drive the operation underground and have little effect in achieving any measure of eradication.

We have, therefore, decided not to fold our arms and wait for government action against the practice, and have launched a massive campaign of education and persuasion against the practice. We believe that most of our African women are suffering under the ignorance of traditional practices and dying of diseases because of a lack of practical information that could change their lives. We campaign by sending our field staff and workers to each home in every community to educate the occupants on the evils of genital mutilations. Our campaigners go on countryside enlightenment tours and address women in public places—anywhere that they may be seen, such as roadsides and markets—on the problems of the practice. We also campaign with literature and newspapers, and on radio and television. Although some women who are disabled by the practice are sometimes in our campaign team, we have never shown them in public as such, in order not to expose them to shame and disgrace.

So far, we are making steady progress, for we have been able to cover 100,000 square kilometres of our countryside and have met with five million rural women, whom we have persuaded to refrain from the practice. All the women that we have met, and especially the youngsters, have shown their willingness to refrain from the practice and have appreciated our work. We have also contacted two million women by radio and television, and another two million through our newspaper and literature. Arrangements have also been completed for the launching of the campaign in other African countries when funds are available.

However, there are some problems that have beset our campaign efforts. There are some traditionalists who accuse our campaigners of being "traitors to women" by exposing the shameful practice of our women to the outside world. Some of those traditionalists are midwives who depend on genital mutilation for their livelihood. Moreover, there is no African leader at the present time, be he socialist, communist, capitalist, or military dictator, who has spoken against the operations. African governments are insensitive to the issue and have not been willing to support any campaign effort with funding. Our greatest problem is lack of sufficient funds. But, in the face of these difficulties, we still continue to fight for changes in the future, so that female circumcision will no longer be an accepted and widespread practise.

FOOTNOTES

1 Fran Hosken, "Female Sexual Mutilations: The Facts and Proposals for Action," *Win News* (1980), p. 55.
2 Genesis 17:10, *The Bible, Revised Standard Version*.
3 Hosken, "Female Sexual Mutilations ..." p. 56.
4 Women's Centre, Box 185, Eket Akwa Ibom State, Nigeria, unpublished manuscript, 1987.

BEAUTY QUESTS—A DOUBLE DISSERVICE
Beguiled, Beseeched and Bombarded— Challenging the Concept of Beauty

Lesley Hall
AUSTRALIA

WHEN I WAS SIXTEEN I paid my last visit to an orthopaedic surgeon. He wanted to carve me up, perform a miracle on my body and transform me into a normal person. But, this time, I intended to say no. I thought of how I should tell him this. After six years, I was tired of the miracle cures that never worked. My body was functioning as it had when I was nine years old, before they started working on me. I did not want to lose what it had taken so long to regain.

I went into the doctor's office hoping that I would have the guts to reject this operation. It was a carrot that the medical profession kept dangling before my eyes.

I did not have to make the decision. The operation was not appropriate for my disability. The surgeon was not going to perform it. He was apologetic. My disability would worsen and he was sorry because he knew it was ugly.

His accusation confronted me. He had called me ugly. There was more to beauty than wearing makeup and stockings, or the right clothes. I was ugly and not because my legs were too skinny, my bust undeveloped, or my face too plain. I was ugly because I was a disabled person. I was ugly and I would get uglier as my disability progressed.

Until then, beauty was a quality I had aspired to. Along with other females of my age, I poured over the magazines. I was fashion conscious, although the clothes I chose often made me look more hideous. I did these things not because I enjoyed doing them—mostly I did not—but because I wanted to prove something to the world.

I was a woman. My lipsticks and stockings and psychedelic dresses would prove it. Being a woman I would be entitled to the privileges and successes that came with womanhood. That success would come my way, with a marriage and children and a job, I never doubted. I knew I had to compete with other women. But I thought I could do it. I had been conditioned as a girl. It was a conditioning that had been the same as the conditioning of other females.

Every day of our lives women are beseeched with the concept of beauty. Baby girls are called pretty and dressed in frills. As we grow older we are told to stay cleaner than our brothers, we learn what is ladylike behaviour. Puberty continues this process, as new aromas are being neutralized, and modesty encouraged. The dreaded blood spot becomes an obsession as we learn to hate our bodies.

The blooming of womanhood reveals a flower that is plucked and then repainted and deodorized, then perfumed, padded and constricted, and pulled into and out of every shape in order to approximate the mythical concept of beauty. This bombardment continues until the day of our death.

Women are told that beauty is equivalent to success. Success in marriage, career, family and relationships depends on using the right lipstick, wearing the right clothes, using deodorants and tampons.

We have an image to conform to. Aspiring to this image necessitates competing with other women. Both the image and the competition is reinforced by advertisements and by "beauty quests" (also known as beauty pageants). Beauty quests are the epitome of competition.

There are many beauty quests held each year throughout Australia. They include baby shows, junior competitions, competitions for married women, country show girls and teenage queens, brides of the year, queens of festivals and Miss Suburbans. There is a "Miss Whatever" to respond to most stages of a female's development. These quests ensure that females will be judged against a concept of beauty, against the other contestants and against all other women. While there are particular qualities in each quest that may differ in respect to the differing age groups that they cater for, they all perform the same role of judging contestants against the prevailing norm of what a female of that age, background, and marital status should conform to.

Some of the quests attempt to play down this setting of standards, because of the criticisms that feminists and disability rights activists have levelled against them in recent years. In particular the Miss Australia Quest denies that it is a beauty quest. Yet fat women never win it—one of the criteria for judging is beauty of figure. Women with disfigured faces do not win—another criteria is beauty of face.

One recent winner in Victoria has a birth mark on her nose. But you cannot see it because she disguises it with makeup. After she won the contest she decided to come out with her secret. She thought that winning, despite her defect, would be an inspiration to disabled women and that it would prove you do not need to be perfect to enter and win a beauty quest.

Yet her actions proved the opposite. She has known the stigma attached to having a defective body and she has learned that to be successful she must hide her blemish. She is telling disabled women that we will succeed too if we hide our defects. But I cannot camouflage the hump on my back by using makeup. Disabled women cannot remove the stigma of their disabilities by simply using cosmetics. To assist women who are disabled this woman should not cover up her birth mark. She should challenge the concepts of beauty and success that make her hide her defect and she should insist the world accept her as she is. By wearing makeup to hide this mark she is reinforcing the stereotype of beauty and telling us that success for a woman only comes by hiding your real self. She is saying that to be disfigured is to be second rate. This is an attitude that disabled women reject.

In challenging what is beautiful we have recognized that all women suffer. The looks, figures, deportment and posture of every woman is scrutinized daily. We are measured against an ideal. Is our hair blonde, are we too fat, too thin, too old, do we walk with the right gait, are our clothes fashionable? A quick glance adds these things up and an assessment is made. We are rated as "a good sort," "an old bag," "a bit of alright." We are defined and categorized according to our looks.

Most women know the frustration of not shaping up, of dieting, shaving legs, wearing makeup, of accentuating good points, of hiding and camouflaging bad ones.

For women who are disabled this problem becomes insurmountable. We cannot diet away our disabilities or cover a disfigured face with makeup, or disguise an epileptic seizure. We cannot wear our ill-fitting clothes with panache when our disability gives us a drunken appearance. We are not contenders in the beauty stakes. Our disabilities have made us outcasts from womanhood. And because we do not line up in this quest for beauty we are discriminated against even further.

"But beauty is in the eye of the beholder," we are told. "It is beauty underneath that counts," we are told. These are the lies that we are told.

The beholder of the eye is most often the man who decides if we get a job, a house, a bank loan, the contraceptive pill. From where does he get his opinion? How does he know that my degree of thinness isn't fashionable? He knows because he is told constantly by advertisements and by beauty quests.

Beauty quests teach people to judge appearances. They not only set the standards of the day but they also enforce them. Women are encouraged to pit their beauty against other women to find out who is the fairest. Being a beautiful woman will often bring many rewards.

Those of us who are not beautiful, who have seen through the mask of beauty and have cast it aside by opposing beauty quests are called envious, sour grapes, a range of names which not only underline the importance of beauty but also highlight the true nature of beauty quests.

When men look at disabled women they judge us on our sexual attractiveness. Being disabled, we do not rate highly. When women judge us, their attitudes are formed by their conditioning as nurturers.

Women are the offenders in the sympathy trade. It is women who run the auxiliaries, raise the money, organize the charity events. It is women who are the do-gooders, who patronize and feel sorry for the poor unfortunate ... It is women who have swallowed the message of charity. It is a message which is aimed straight at the duality of women's conditioned qualities—to care about and do unto others. These qualities are seen plainly in the young country women who enter the various beauty quests. Their sense of doing good is sharply contrasted to the attitudes of the city models and public relations women. The commitment of the country women is real, their desire to improve people's lives is genuine, but their actions are misguided.

They are misguided because they do nothing to help the people in their own communities. The money that they raise goes to large institutionalized organizations that are city-based. Many disabled people who wish to use these services must leave their local communities. The raising of money does nothing to maintain or return disabled people to their own homes. The fundraising does not help disabled people get work or use the local swimming pool or recreational facility.

In order to raise the money for these institutionalized services, disabled people are presented as childlike and in need of the public's pity. This creates negative impressions in people's minds. Disabled people become poor unfortunates.

Being disabled is being different. To be disabled is to face experiences which are different from those of non-disabled people. For many people it involves institutionalization and segregation from the mainstream of the community in education, work, housing and leisure activities. It means being on the receiving end of prejudice and discrimination.

Prejudice and discrimination are based on appearances. People are judged not on their ability but on the way they look. Disabled people look different from other people. The difference is caused by disability. Discrimination results when this difference triggers the negative attitudes towards disability that are held by the other person.

Attitudes towards disability are not formed accidently. They are the obvious outcome of a society that values competition between people. People are judged according to their success in education, work, marriage, by their ability to produce (healthy) offspring, by their creativity and beauty. As a result of our segregation, disabled people have fewer opportunties to acquire the skills necessary for a good job. Our education is substandard; we have less access to housing and other services.

Because of our segregation, most people form their attitudes towards us by internalizing the message of charity. People who are not disabled will only form positive attitudes to disabled people when they meet us in everyday life. For this to occur, integrated services must be established to enable disabled people to participate in all of the community's activities.

In addition, we must cease to be judged on our appearances. Competitions which set and enforce standards of beauty must be abolished. It is for these reasons that women who are disabled oppose beauty quests.

Beauty quests force on us a standard of appearance. Because of our disabilities, this standard is impossible to attain. Everytime we are judged against it we inevitably fail. We become second-class women.

Beauty quests that raise money in the name of disabled people do us a double disservice. Through patronizing fundraising activities, the community sees again and again that we are "inferior" people. Disabled people will only gain an equal place within society when our services are fully integrated. People in the community must be allowed to develop positive attitudes towards us. The abolition of beauty quests will be a significant step towards this end.

DRAWING

Trudy Clutterbak
Australia

CROSSING THE HIGH COUNTRY

Amber Coverdale Sumrall
UNITED STATES

THE NARROW TRAIL INTO Round Lake winds up and over a high mountain pass in a series of steep switchbacks. The morning air is cool and sharp; it stings when I inhale. This is my first backpacking trip since I lost my leg fourteen years ago in an auto accident. I climb slowly, methodically, not yet acclimated to the altitude. I wear a below-the-knee prosthesis on my right leg and a foot brace on my left. I am aware of every stone, every piece of wood on the path. One false step, one twist of my ankle or knee and I would have to be carried out of the Sierra Nevadas. For leverage and balance I use a gnarled branch of madrone as a walking stick.

I have been walking and practicing yoga for weeks in preparation for this. On my back is a daypack, stuffed with my sleeping bag and a dozen wool stump socks. A pair of field glasses for bird-observing hang from my neck. My husband, John, carries forty pounds of gear on his back.

"You set the pace," he tells me, following several steps behind. "You'll get to flush the birds too." He has hoped ever since we met that I would someday be able to experience the high country and is prepared to do anything to make this possible. We will walk for five miles, then make camp.

I have known John for over eight years. The fact that I am an amputee made not the slightest difference to him when we met. It does now, though. When I limp through the house, steeped in self-pity, and loathing my "condition," as he calls it, his patience wears thin. "Everything's conditional," he says, the way the hippies used to say, "everything's relative." John thinks I should have a hut to go to at these times, modelled on the menstrual huts of Native American women. A quiet, solitary place to reflect and heal. He refuses to indulge my self-destructive moods but will massage my foot, back, neck, legs, whenever I am in pain.

It is early morning in the Sierras, the sun has not yet crossed the snow-capped peaks. Robins and purple finches punctuate the silence with song. Across the valley patches of snow are melting, becoming streams that feed Woods and Winnemucca Lakes.

Last week I had the screws tightened in my artificial foot and bought a new pair of hiking boots. At the last minute I decided in favour of my old, well-broken-in work boots. As we climb up the mountain my artifical foot begins to creak. So much for sneaking up on birds, I think, wondering if this leg is going the way of my last one.

At an art exhibit, several years ago, I found myself falling mysteriously in slow motion. I grabbed onto a table of leather-bound journals to stop my descent but they tumbled down with me. I noticed that my foot was hanging by a thread from the rest of my prosthesis. It swung back and forth like a pendulum. A crowd formed in record time, unable to comprehend that this was not a flesh and blood foot.

"Is she drunk?" someone asked, in response to my wild laughter at their horrified expressions. "Drunk or crazy," some-one else replied, as I sat on the floor wondering how to escape the pandemonium. A fellow amputee, sensing what had occurred, pushed through the crowd and carried me to my car. It was worth the discomfort and embarrassment to see the shock register on all those faces as they stared at my rapidly swivelling foot. I felt as if this was my initiation into a secret, esoteric club. Able-bodied need not apply.

At the summit of Meese Pass we stop to rest. I gulp air greedily, attempting to make up for the reduced oxygen. The rising sun has illuminated the meadow below and for as far as I can see there are wild blue iris, bright yellow mules ears and purple lupine. I remove my outer flannel shirt, change my stump sock, which is wet and hot. I will have to change socks every thirty minutes to prevent blisters and sores. They slip easily through the loop on my pack and will dry in the breeze while we walk.

Clark's nutcrackers dart from tree to tree, collecting pine nuts from Jeffrey pines as we enter a series of meadows, threaded with tiny streams. I want to come back as a bird. To choose whether to walk or to fly. It is no coincidence that my dreams of flying have increased lately; I have been so frustrated with the sheer effort of moving my body from place to place. It seems that as soon as my ankle recovers from tendonitis, or my sciatica is in remission, my stump develops a painful pressure sore which necessitates hours of not wearing my prosthesis. Flying appears to be so effortless.

It is a rare occurrence that I'm not dealing with some imbalance in my body. Most of the time I am able to take this in stride and chalk up more writing time (sitting at my desk requires no great energy expenditure other than tremendous willpower). But on the bad days I internalize anger and contempt for my body as if it were the enemy, plotting my demise. When the simple act of walking down to my garden for tomatoes or squash irritates my ankle or stump or both, I become afraid and withdraw. The "how could anyone ever want to put up with me" mantra resonates through my head and the familiar fear of dependency wells up to such an extent that I refuse to answer the phone or reach out to my friends. I clump around the house ranting and raving like a madwoman and even my cats avoid me.

John and I stop at the headwaters of the Truckee River to wash our faces. Removing my prosthesis, I check for redness and bathe my leg. From this point it is all downhill to Round Lake, through sub-alpine meadows then forests of red and white fir. Dozens of woodpeckers, warblers, Lazuli buntings and nuthatches flit overhead and the rising warm fragrance of crunched pine needles beneath our feet permeates the air. Finally, we pass through a dense canopy of Lodgepole pine to arrive in a beaver's marsh bordered by a quaking aspen grove.

"The lake's just beyond those trees," John says. "I'll scout the easiest way in. How are you doing?"

"I'm exhausted, ready to eat."

"Yeah, me too. It's the altitude."

He sheds his pack and disappears beyond the aspen grove. Unstrapping my prosthesis, I check again for swelling or irritation. The air temperature is cool at this elevation, a critical factor. My stump is fine.

"There is no simple way down," John says on his return. "We have to make our own train from this point. There are lots of rocks to climb over."

Slowly, we pick our way across the maze of granite boulders. This is extremely difficult for me, my artificial foot is not flexible, does not yield to the surface beneath it. It wedges in the small clefts between boulders. When we arrive, hand in hand, at our chosen campsite there are no other people at the lake. We have the water, the birds, the fish, all the beauty of this place to ourselves. Above us are pinnacles of vertical rimrock, eroded into strange formations, lifting from the lake. A perfect nesting site for Golden Eagles and Red-tailed Hawks.

Two days ago, when John was working on our sauna, I told him I was ready to go to Round Lake and he said he'd take time off. I first heard about this magical place from him—he'd been here long ago. My decision was not a conscious one. Rather, my body gave signals that it was capable and I responded, trusting as I have recently learned to do, in its innate wisdom.

Last spring, when I was putting in my garden, I refused to stop digging and shovelling dirt when my stump began to hurt, needing to go beyond the pain, to "overcome" it. As a result I was unable to wear my prosthesis for days afterwards. I used crutches and a wheelchair. In retrospect I like to think it was a conspiracy of body/mind/spirit to start me writing again. I do not need to incapacitate myself in order to work at my poems and prose now, although I prefer doing almost anything, including cleaning the birdcage, to approaching my desk.

After a short rest, during which several Mountain chickadees and Stellar's jays check us out, we pitch the tent and hang our food to keep it safe from bears and raccoons. Choosing the perfect rock overlooking the lake, we devour our lunch of hardboiled eggs, trail mix and bananas. It's true what John says—*anything* tastes gourmet after hours of hiking.

His sense of humour tends towards slapstick but he has never hidden my leg as a practical joke even when he knows I am liable to ruin his morning on any given day, by following him around the kitchen with a full list of grievances. When I kicked the basement door in, totally enraged after the third of three custom-made prostheses in one month didn't fit, he calmly stuffed the jagged hole with newspaper. Later, he transformed one of them into a planter, filled with forget-me-nots, for my birthday.

Tossing the last of the trail mix to the juncoes, we make our way down to a slab of smooth granite at water's edge. John unpacks his fishing reel and baits a hook with silver lures to attract cutthroat trout. Shedding my clothes, I stretch out in the hot sun, close my eyes and listen to the whir of the reel.

A week ago I was a Tassajara Hot Springs, east of Big Sur, California. Women of many ages and sizes lay naked together on the deck by the creek. I felt shy when I took off my clothes; even when I did not observe them looking I felt their eyes on me, their unspoken questions. As I entered the steambath with my friend, Dena, who carried my prosthesis in and out (it's not waterproof) as I needed it, one of the women asked about my leg. When I told her about the accident she took both my hands in hers, looked me in the eyes and said, "Thank you for the courage and beauty you bring to this place."

I did not grow up loving my body. The messages I received, as an able-bodied Catholic girl in the '50s, were consistent in their negativity. My body was considered a temple of the Holy Ghost, on loan from God, to be held in trust like a gold certificate until I died. A woman was classified as virgin, whore, or mother. How to get from virgin to mother and still have a good time was a dilemma for many of us. I opted for becoming a tomboy.

As I outgrew the Church I learned to add and subtract points for hair, skin, eyes, teeth, mouth, breasts etc. seeing myself as the sum of my parts, believing that if my life wasn't working it was because of my low score. My beloved grandmother, Nellie June, did her utmost to convince me that I was the most splendid young woman she knew. Hers was the lone voice of absolute acceptance and love. I didn't buy it until after she died.

If able-bodied women can't accept their bodies how do they view their disabled sisters? And, more importantly, how do we view ourselves? The great white homogeneous society sees women as sex objects or they don't see us at all. Disabled women are perceived neither as sexual beings nor as invisible. In a world of commodities we are "damaged goods."

It is a relief to be the square peg in a round hole actually. To defy the labels and stereotypes. To be the tomboy again. So that at Tassajara, when I sit among women, naked and vulnerable, it perhaps frees each of us to accept our own bodies a little more.

Sliding off the rock into the icy water I swim over to the beaver dam that we walked across a few hours ago, a bridge of aspen limbs, mud and dried grasses. It appeared so fragile I couldn't believe it would support us. Water hyacinth pads float across the lake; lazily I glide among them as John lifts fish from the water.

As the afternoon shifts to evening we return to our clothes and gather wood for the campfire. John prepares dinner: pan-fried trout, rice, and cheddar-cauliflower soup. The stars appear, one by one, the Big Dipper directly overhead. We drink hot chocolate as the flames die down, relaxing into the serenity of this place. My entire body aches but it is a good ache, muscles exerted to their capacity. As the moon rises we bed down in the tent, sleeping bags zipped together, our bodies twined around one another.

The loss of my limb did not affect my sexuality. I decided after the accident, at age twenty-eight, that anyone who would reject me on purely physical grounds was not someone I'd care to be lovers with. Because I could now "pass" as an able-bodied woman most of the time it was often a shock for a potential lover to learn of my disability. I confess to a perverse delight in witnessing people's reactions over the years. John is fond of saying, "It's not how you're built, it's how you're wired."

Something wakes me in the night, a receding sound close to the tent like a large animal scuttling away through the woods. I imagine it is a bear, can't get back to sleep. There is always some fear to deal with, tangible or intangible. Ultimately, it is the fear of dying that permeates all the others. I believe that those who are most threatened by disabled persons are those who do not acknowledge their own mortality. Those of us who are disabled are continual reminders of nature's random workings. I prefer to think of those who are not disabled as *temporarily* able-bodied, for sooner or later most of us will experience a major disability. Not many of us die in our sleep these days.

Just as our society views the aging/dying process as an adversary, so it also views the disabled person as "other." This distancing leads to apathy, which leads, inevitably, as in the case of some Third World peoples, to eventual genocide. Anyone or anything that threatens the patriarchal, imperialist structure's need to dominate and control is perceived as a threat. Including nature. Including strong life-affirming women.

At first light I awaken again to the raucous sounds of a Clark's nutcracker picking through the ashes of last night's fire. It flies off with a small clump of rice. There are days when I feel like such a scavenger. Days when my stump retains water before my period, and my prosthesis will not fit properly. Days when my ankle will not support me. I am like the bird, searching for sustenance among the ashes. Sometimes I manage to pull something out: a book, a remembered chunk of advice, a phone call to a friend, the appearance of a special bird at my feeder, a poem that surfaces, or the stunning beauty of the day itself.

After breakfast of trout and eggs, and one last swim, we prepare for the long hike out. My clean stump socks are drying on a rock; I loop them through the pack. They will dry as I walk. It is noon, very warm and an uphill climb most of the way. I need to stop frequently: to rest, drink from the canteen, change socks. It takes over four hours to reach our car at the trailhead. I allow my body to carry me slowly, to take the time it needs.

At the place where the mountain pass levels out and the switchbacks end there is a wooden plank crossing a stream. Lush plants spring up on either side. The plants and herbs are unfamiliar but their fragrance is a blend of citrus, lavender and, perhaps, sage. An image of my grandmother's bedroom comes to mind. Of course, it is the way her room smelled when I visited. The mixture of sachet, dusting powder and orange blossoms from her fruit trees outside. She has come from the spirit world to greet me here. Her words echo down the canyon, "Honeygirl, if you listen to your own inner voice you'll never go wrong." My grandma, with her wisdom and Mohawk connections to the earth taught me to believe in myself. I silently give thanks for her blessing, for this crossing.

As John and I pull shoes, socks, dirty jeans off by the car I am already contemplating my next adventure. I want to participate in the upcoming blocade at Concord Naval Weapons Station. As a sanctuary activist this is an issue close to my heart. Because I need my arms free, for equilibrium, I cannot allow myself to be handcuffed. A wheelchair is the only alternative. This means I will leave my prothesis at home. I am afraid of being so vulnerable, so dependent on others. I am scared and uneasy and I am going to do it anyway. For Nellie June, for all disabled women, for myself.

V

DEALING WITH THE WORLD

It [the seminar] helped me and others gain a feeling of unity with other people with disabilities. Sometimes it feels like it's only me, but there are disabled people all over the world ... You tend to draw strength from each other.

— Marie McQueen *Guyana*
(Interview with Diane Driedger, July 21, 1988, Roseau, Dominica, at the Women in Development Leadership Training Seminar, sponsored by Disabled Peoples' International).

This is an exciting time. Groups and networks of women with disabilities are organizing all over the world ... Governments everywhere are beginning to listen to us.

— Pat Israel *Canada*
("Keynote Address," *National Organizing Meeting of the DisAbled Women's Network, DAWN, Report, March 26-29, 1987, Winnipeg, Canada.* Vancouver: DAWN Canada, 1987.)

CONFRONTED WITH ATTITUDINAL and physical barriers, women with disabilities around the world are challenging the system that holds the barriers in place. Self-help and advocacy groups of women with disabilities have sprung up on every continent to call for changes. And women have undertaken their own individual battles to overturn the barriers that oppress them. Indeed, the women who write in this section are all successfully dealing with the world.

Rosemary Webb of Northern Ireland tells of her life as a

woman with a disability and the effect upon her of joining a group of disabled persons who provide peer support and lobby for access to public facilities. Similarly, Gerda Kloske writes about the history of blind women in Germany and relates how they have begun to organize and provide support for each other.

T. Christina F. Stummer of Brazil describes her experience of disability and discusses the personal activism that led to her obtaining an education. She then tells of her experience with disabled activists in France and her membership in a group of disabled persons in Brazil.

Gem Wirszilas traces the birth and growth of the DisAbled Women's Network (DAWN) Canada. She relates her own story of disability and her growth, and the growth of other women, as they banded together in a DAWN British Columbia chapter. zana of the United States adds drawings of two women with disabilities sharing their strength.

Maria Cristina Mathiason of Austria discusses her experience as a woman with a disability living in both "developed" and "developing" countries. She has faced barriers in both environments and found, in the end, that she was empowered by her involvement in Disabled Peoples' International at the United Nations.

Judy Heumann relates how her own struggle to obtain the right to become a teacher in New York started a movement of disabled people for change. One voice for change became many voices. She discusses her role in starting the first Centre for Independent Living in the United States.

Finally, Lesley Hall of Australia describes her experiences forming a feminist group of women with disabiities, which became a support group and also a force for change, advocating against beauty pageants and publishing a book of writings by women with disabilities. In the end she proclaims that women, together, will decide what *is* ...

LIFE HAS BEEN GIVEN TO ALL OF US

Rosemary Webb
NORTHERN IRELAND, UNITED KINGDOM

NORTHERN IRELAND. I WONDER WHAT these two words conjure up in your mind? Perhaps nothing at all. We are a very small island with a history that goes back many hundreds of years—to the days before the great Cuchulain (pronounced, "Cahool-an") and "The Knights of the Red Branch" who dedicated themselves to defend Ulster (one of the four Provinces of Ireland; Munster, Leinster and Connaught being the other three) against her "enemies." Cuchulain's mother was a sister of King Connor of Ireland, and there were many deeds of bravery performed by Cuchulain, not only in Ireland, but also in Scotland.

This all happened before Christianity came to Ireland, brought by St. Patrick, who as a boy tended sheep on the hillside of Slemish Mountain, which is within sight of the house in which I now live in County Antrim. St. Patrick died on March 17 in the year 461 AD.

The poet John Donne wrote many years later, "Any man's death diminishes me," and, alas, in this beautiful island of Ireland in this present day we do see the sad and devastating loss of life.

Ireland is indeed a lovely place, from its rocky coastline in the North, to the soft misty mountains of Mourne on the East coast, made more famous by a poet, the late Percy French, in his song, "Where the Mountains of Mourne Sweep Down to the Sea." Travelling on to Georgian Dublin, to the west coast of Kerry, there is beauty everywhere.

I live in Northern Ireland, which has six counties, and is largely rural, except for the cities of Belfast and Londonderry. My young days were spent in Belfast, where I was born into a happy family—my father was a hard-working doctor, born in Ulster, and my mother was of Scottish descent. Discipline was strict, but did me no harm. I attended a day school and grew up a normal healthy girl. I was not academic; my love was for games and sport of every kind—tennis, golf, badminton, lacrosse, netball, swimming, roller and ice skating, fencing—and team games which offered fun and hard training.

I married young, and my three daughters were all born while I was in my early twenties. My husband lived in the country, and I was very happy to live in a rural community. As our children grew to be teenagers, I took up voluntary work in addition to looking after my ducks, turkeys and vegetable garden. I became a prison visitor, and was appointed a Lay Magistrate on a local Juvenile Court Panel, where I served for many years. I also joined a committee of a large special care hospital for physically and mentally handicapped children and young people.

I became interested in juvenile remand homes for boys and girls, visiting and working on their committees. Life was very busy and very full and I had the honour of becoming Chief Commissioner of County Antrim Girl Guides. It was at this time I began to have walking difficulties, and after many tests trouble with my spine was diagnosed. I had a fall at home, broke my thigh, and spent three months in a Belfast hospital where I also had a benign tumour removed from my spine.

In my usual optimistic way, after discharge from the hospital I was sure I would be back to my busy life in a few months. However, things did not work out as I had hoped. I had been left with a weak right leg, and walking became more and more difficult in spite of months of physiotherapy, exercises and perseverance.

Arthritis and several slipped discs in my spine necessitated that I use crutches to get about, and later on, a wheelchair. I had my car adapted and learned to use a hand accelerator and brake; my car is my lifeline to the outside world. Though we moved into a different house, we still live in a semi-rural area. My daughters all married and two families moved to England where it was easier to find work. I had a Home Help four hours a week to help with housework and any shopping I could not do.

Sadly, at this time, my husband died and I was on my own. Because of my growing disablement, I had to give up much of the voluntary work I had been doing, and I looked around for those things I could do. As I lived alone, I felt it necessary to get out and mix with people. I joined the Antrim and Randalstown Physically Handicapped Group locally. Antrim and Randalstown are small towns—Antrim has about 35,000 people and Randalstown's population is a little less—and we have men and women from both towns in our group. When the group was started by two occupational therapists about ten years ago, there were about twenty members. Now, not many of the original people are there; over the years they have moved away or become worse in health. New members arrive from time to time. We have about fifteen members at the moment and we meet one day each month. Unfortunately, our weekly meeting had to be cancelled due to cuts in the bus service which conveyed the minibus to the Day Centre. Even now we hear of further difficulties and are doing all we can to keep our group going. During this past summer we have been able to hire a bus for day outings and have enjoyed several all-day excursions. For a nominal sum we travel about eighty to one hundred miles. During autumn and winter months we have discussions—speakers and slides on wildlife, flowers and travel. Each year our Group tries to give some donation to a group of people less fortunate than ourselves. In the past we have been able, by having cake sales and by other means, to raise enough to give towards a kidney unit in City Hospital, Belfast; the Heart Unit at the Waveney Hospital, Ballymena; the Chest, Heart and Stroke Association; a new Children's Cancer Unit in the Children's Hospital and a Leukemia Unit. This past year we were able to give £300 to the Northern Ireland Hospice.

We are hoping to join up with the Physically Handicapped and Able-Bodied Group to lobby for "access." This is a subject that affects us all.

Over the last ten years or so many improvements for disabled people have taken place in Northern Ireland. I have personally been loaned, by the District Health and Social Services, aids which assist my lifestyle, among which are a hard mattress, a wheelchair and crutches, and a bath with a post screwed into the floor and a chair attached which swings out and then across the bath. I also have had a ramp put in at the high step of my back door. All these allow me to live alone and keep my independence.

At present, I am negotiating for a "Removable Electric Boot Lift" for my wheelchair that will lift my folded chair into the boot [or trunk] of my car, and take it out again. This will give me complete independence as I always have to enlist the help of people to lift my chair out and put it back into the car for me. This, of course, will be my own property.

In the British Isles, people with walking difficulties or who are virtually unable to walk, can—on the recommendation of their doctor—be supplied with a stick-on Orange Badge for their car. This enables them to use parking facilities reserved for disabled persons. Though stores and public buildings have a few parking spaces for Orange Badge cars, they are quite often filled with cars belonging to non-disabled drivers. In England such people have to pay quite a heavy fine, in Northern Ireland they do not.

If I wish to visit the Belfast Opera House and have my Orange Badge on my car, I must be in the precincts of the Opera House at least one-and-a-half hours before the doors open. In spite of many requests for them to provide one or two parking spaces for Orange Badge holders, this has been persistently refused. Perhaps we should understand this, for many thousands of pounds were spent recently restoring this splendid building, which one car bomb could destroy in a matter of moments.

A member of our local disabled group found out that all the dentists in the town had their surgeries upstairs. She brought this to the attention of the District Health Committee. They were able to make arrangements with the dentists whereby any disabled person could be seen at the local Health Centre, which is all on ground level.

Some of us have been instrumental in asking our churches to put up a hand rail beside entrance steps to the church. We have had pavements lowered in the town. They are difficult, not only for disabled people, but for prams and the elderly. We were able to have parking spaces put in our local shopping centre car park—but this took two years! And spaces were not in the place we had wanted.

Our local disabled group, of which I am Secretary, felt that the main shopping area of our town was now so crowded that we could not get our cars to the curb of the pavement. We communicated with the Traffic Branch of the police and the Roads Division of the Department of the Environment, to see if we could have a parking bay for cars. As vehicles cannot be left unattended, someone is normally left in the car for a couple of hours, but a concession has been made for Orange Badge holders, provided they leave a note as to where they are and a cardboard clock stating the time they left the car. A lot of small towns have different by-laws. Our request seemed to have no end in sight and after one year we asked for help from the Northern Ireland Council on Disability. The result was a conference in the Police Station, where three of us in wheelchairs and an access officer stated our case to representatives from both the Police and the Roads Division. And once again we were refused a parking bay. But the authorities did offer us Traffic Wardens, who would patrol the street, moving cars on, and not allowing double parking. After two years, we have now got our Traffic Wardens and this has eased traffic for everyone—however, the victory did take patience and per-severance.

I still manage one or two committees, which meet monthly. On the Cheshire Home Committee, we are building accommodation for young physically handicapped people, who will live in their own flats with kitchens and bathrooms, and go to work from there. This is paid for by subscriptions from the public and Borough Councils. There is a warden on the premise should assistance be required. For the last five or six years I have attended as a student in the Extramural Department of Queen's University, Belfast, studying a wide variety of subjects. I may have to forego the next session, though, because my pain is increasing and the journey to Belfast in my car is becoming more arduous.

What do people like myself, who have a limited lifestyle but once enjoyed complete independence, miss most? I found at the beginning of my disablement that it is wise to realize what one's limitations are, and to try not to overstep them too often. I certainly miss long walks along a sandy bay with sea spray on my face, and a swim in the cold sea. I miss golf and tennis, and shopping alone from store to store, choosing and picking out my needs, spending a whole day in the large Belfast shops. (I do incidentally take my wheelchair and shop alone locally in the shopping centre, which is all on one level.) It would be good to be able to dress in the morning without pain—and in a matter of minutes as I used to—and not have to leave myself so much time to get anywhere.

Many people travel the world in their wheelchairs. I am afraid pain deters me from going too far afield now. But I did visit friends in Toronto, Canada in the 1970s and was most impressed at the pride taken by the citizens in their town, and at the thoughtful planning for disabled people. It seemed so enlightened and forward looking, making it practical for disabled people to visit anywhere in their city. I visit one daughter in England also, and find the airline staff more than helpful when they have a person in a wheelchair.

I hope that more progress can be made so that disabled people can be integrated into the community. None of us wishes to have special treatment, but we do need access and aids to make life easier and more balanced.

I cannot finish without mentioning the generosity and kindness of the Northern Ireland people. Perhaps this may sound diametrically opposed to the life that goes on around us, and which you see on your television screens, but it is true all the same. Help is forthcoming from those from whom we least expect it. And disablement has no barriers in religion, race or colour, for life has been given to all of us, to live to our highest expectations.

EVERYTHING IS IN MOTION

Gerda Kloske
A Representative of the Blind Women
Organized in the German Federation of the Blind
GERMANY

THROUGH THE AGES, BLIND people, particularly blind women, have led their lives aimlessly as the illiterates, beggars and pariahs of their societies. Over time, however, even blind women have secured a firm status within the social system.

Blind people had no influence in shaping cultural development. We did not belong to the strata of people of action—conquerors and rulers. We used to rank even below the slaves, the outlaws and the serfs. The serfs had an economic value, because they carried the burden of unpaid labour and were an appendage to the property just like cattle. If blind people, despite these miserable conditions, were not starving to death, it was for the sole reason that people were afraid that this cruel fate might one day affect them too. Thus, they gave alms to blind persons. Happy was a girl in those days if her figure was good and her looks graceful, because she could find work as a prostitute. Prostitution was probably the oldest profession for blind women. Girls with glaucoma were in especially great demand because of their beautiful, big eyes.

The Greek philosopher, Heraclitus, who lived around 500 BC, is believed to have said: "Panta rhei," a Greek term which means "Everything is in continuous flow."[1] At some times it flows slowly, at others fast. Slowly, very slowly indeed, did those destinies flow which were to shape the history of blind people. "Verehrt, ernahrt, bewahrt" (revered, fed, approved)! These three catchwords are commonly used to refer to the stages of evolution of the blind people's movement. Like all catchwords, however, they contain generalizations, some partly true, some partly false. Certainly, in the ancient days, a few blind men were indeed held in reverence. But these were individuals such as philosophers, poets and, most prominently, bards, who were the bearers of the religious and historical tradition. Theresias the bard, and Homer the philosopher come to mind. At all times there have been excellent blind men like these, not just in antiquity. But where were the blind women? How dreary! They suffered from famine and were in want. Frequently blind women were murdered because of their vain existence.

The teachings of Jesus Christ brought about a change in culture, although for many years they failed to bear fruits for blind people. True, the religious doctrine, "Everybody is your fellow creature," made us a part of society. Although we basically remained beggars for a very long time, the looks cast upon us perhaps lost some of the anger they used to have; after all, we, too, were brothers and sisters.

In the Middle Ages, not much changed. Blind persons were considered imbeciles and thus were not fit for education and work. We were dependent on the charity and generosity of benevolent sovereigns and the help provided by the church and cloisters. The idea that by performing acts of clemency the individual would secure for him or herself a place in heaven was widely held.

With the advent of humanism, only a faint dawn was discernible on the horizon. Gradually, a change was occurring. The Government recognized that all people, including blind people, had the same rights to education and humanism. There was no knowledge, however, of how to translate these insights into action. Education was available only to a small number of blind people who were endowed with much energy and a good family background. We certainly would not know anything about Theresia of Paradies' excellent piano performance had Empress Mary-Therese of Austria not been her godmother.

A new epoch in the inglorious history of blind persons dawned, when, in 1784, Valentin Hauy founded the first educational establishment for blind students. Blind girls, however, were not admitted to the Parisian school. It was the age of the French Revolution, the age of Napoleon, the age of upheaval. The feudal system was giving way to the emerging civic society, which eventually evolved into the welfare state of our time. Throughout

Europe, including Germany and Austria, thirty schools for the blind were opened. In some rare cases, blind girls were also admitted, but by no means did they have equal opportunities. Indeed, in my view, they were just a few of Fortune's favorites.

Eventually, in 1809 Louis Braille, who, in my opinion, is the pre-eminent figure of the 19th century, was born. By creating the six dot system in 1829, he gave us a tactile script (one which is accessible to the sense of touch). Since then, braille has become the central means of communication for blind people worldwide. The first document regarding the educational level of blind persons was not written for fifty years, however. Supervisor Adalbert Stifter commented upon the state of education at the Linz School for the Blind in the year 1853: "According to the view of the undersigned, the education shapes the mind and intellect of the poor miserable souls. They are humanized and given a noble and gentle charm which beautifies their future solitary lives."

For a long period blind people spent their miserable lives inside asylums and were economically dependent on their relatives. If all this was not feasible, the almshouse was the only resort. Still, the blind individual had to pay for this misery with lifelong thankfulness and obedience. This was especially true for blind girls and women. The desire to discard all tutelage and to begin a self-determined, free and responsible life was immense. The chances of realizing this goal were small, not least because it appeared utterly impossible to make a living outside the asylums.

Panta rhei. Friedrich Scherer: We hardly remember his name today. He was a writer, a teacher of the blind and an organizer. With the exception of Louis Braille, he was probably the most important fighter in the nineteenth century for the needs of blind people. Scherer recognized early on that social forces can only evolve if a group organizes. Organizing is a dynamic which, like a wildfire, spreads to all people enabling them to cope with their hard lot. Thus Scherer, together with the ophthalmologist, Albrecht von Grefe, advocated in all parts of Germany for the creation of an organization of blind people. Both men found it difficult to carry out the undertaking. As late as 1874, the first regional self-help organization of blind people was established in Berlin by the blind organist Karl Franz. It took a long time, however, before a national organization of blind persons could speak with one voice for all blind people.

Panta rhei—everything flows again and the twentieth century dawns. Headmaster Kull at the Berlin school for the blind was wondering why blind girls and women should be feeble and ailing. He realized that blind women were under great emotional pressure, because they recognized that in spite of their intellectual abilities and frequent superiority in adroitness, they stood in the shadow of their blind male comrades. Many blind men found a sighted partner at that time and thus found that living with another made, and makes, it easier to cope with blindness. In order to improve the health condition of women, Headmaster Kull created the first recreational homes. Consequently, today's recreational programs, which our male comrades long since have been participating in, originated from Headmaster Kull.

July 1912. The *Reichsdeutscher Blindenverband* is created by 270 men and women in Brunswick as the umbrella organization of blind persons.[2] At that time, being a member in a self-help organization could involve considerable disadvantages. Help from the blind for a blind individual was almost equal to committing a punishable act because the self-help movement, unlike the provision of public and private welfare, was considered impudent and a promotion of special interests. Still, those brave women and men stood by their organization. Their neediness and their mutual lot were the bonds of solidarity uniting them in their struggle for a common cause.

It still took more than sixty years for the modern blind woman to appear. And the blind woman kept on knitting, not just for fun as we do today, but in order to earn her bread. From central locations, cotton and wool were sent to blind women everywhere. Some time later the knitted pieces were sent back to a central organization, the *Allgemeine Blindenverband Berlin*, where they still needed to be sewn together. The knitted goods were completed by well-to-do, upper-class women, who were often members of women's clubs that had come into vogue at the time. Generally, it was sighted people who sold these commodities at welfare events and bazaars. The proceeds which blind women obtained in return were not even the equivalent of pocket-money. But, it was self-earned money, albeit for no more than salt for the soup.

In the 1920s, chair- and brush-making for blind women arrived. Workshops for the blind were created in the form of co-operative societies. Contracts were placed with blind women homeworkers. Gradually, better wages were paid. Those blind women who lived alone had to find the rent for a room and had to live on what they were earning through their hands' work. There was no blindness allowance. The working hours for blind women were seventy or even eighty hours a week. But the blind woman of that time was not discontent with her condition. A blind woman who stood on her own feet—however hard this was—had managed, after all, to rid herself of being patronized within her family, and was independent and alive!

Panta rhei—everything is in motion again. The Second World War invaded the entire globe like a deluge. In 1945, at the close of the terrible and cruel events, blind people, and in particular we, the blind women, were at zero again. There was no work or food. Nor was there any organizational network of associations of the blind, which had proven so powerful a weapon in the blind people's movement and its fight for integration. Starting from the very beginning again took an incredible amount of courage and strength from blind people. Even forty years ago, the desire that had been cherished down through the centuries remained the same. It was blind peoples' desire to have a job, for it is only through working that an independent and self-responsible life becomes possible.

Blind people making crafts was the starting point. Gradually, it became possible to place blind women as industrial workers, masseusses, telephone operators, typists, administrative clerks and academics. Certainly, integration would not have reached the level it has today if thousands of blind people, among them often exemplary blind women, did not mix each day with sighted fellow workers in companies and administrative bodies. Through thousands of years of evolution, we have seen however, how easy it is for a river to change its course.

Panta rhei—we hear and read every day that reorganization for efficiency in industry and unemployment will not stop short at our jobs. But how can things, how *should* things, go on? We are now workers, employees, officials and are working. This involves a commitment from everybody to take more and better action!

There were and still are many qualified female leaders among us: Dr. Friedel Heister, Dr. Fatima Shah, Mrs. Dorina Gouvea Nowill and Dr. Salma Maqbool.[3] To these women we must certainly pay tribute. They have advanced to the highest positions and won recognition.

In the 1970s and 1980s not much progress has been made in improving the status of blind women. In the developing countries there are millions of blind women living in mute misery and who are economically dependent.[4] Neither conferences and congresses nor training seminars held in Europe, Asia and Latin America have helped. The reluctance on the part of most women to take on small civic commitments is a major barrier to blind women's further development.

And this pattern is indeed also true for the blind women of the Federal Republic of Germany. How often I meet women who are lonely, embittered and completely indifferent to what is happening around them, sitting in a corner and saying timidly: "I don't need to have any more." Such women never participate in elections for governments nor in any other activities in their communities. Nobody really knows them. At best, people know that a certain blind woman is said to live somewhere around the community. Our work must start at this very point. For no one shall stand aside or be lonely. I am perfectly aware that this is our top priority, but at the same time it is also the most difficult task of the self-help movement of blind people. Often our efforts must extend over many years until we succeed in getting those women out of their isolation, and in achieving that, they join our groups.

Showing a blind woman the road out of isolation is no easy task.[5] Speaking for myself, I can say that whenever I hear of somebody in our region who has gone blind, I try to encourage her to join our group by visiting her very often at her home and supplying her with information to help her cope better with her situation. I tell her, for instance, what kinds of aids are available for blind people. Training in mobility, and rehabilitation will help a blind woman to move in environments not familiar to her and to handle her duties as a housewife and mother. Most important, however, is to convince the woman that only by becoming a full member of an association of blind persons will she be better able to adapt to her new situation. All this requires one to be prepared at any time of the day or night to answer a person's telephone call whenever she feels down and needs help and consolation. If every one of us attended to just one protegee and led her out of darkness, we would be making a small step forward. If we could also campaign for the removal of negative stereotypes, which often take away our courage to handle matters ourselves, that would be a further, nay, a major step, toward success.

Let me call upon the forty million blind and twenty million visually-impaired people around the world to work for their mutual well-being and to support each other. May there never be a time again when blind people will not be allowed to be active.

FOOTNOTES

1   For a substantial discussion see William K.C. Guthrie, *A History of Greek Philosophy Vol. 1, the Earlier Presocratic and the Pythagoreans,* (Cambridge: The University Press, 1962), pp. 449-469.

2   It should be noted that the Berlin-based *Allgemeiner Blindenverein Berlin* was the first union of blind people at a regional level. Its members were blind individuals whose fixed abode was in Berlin. The *Reichsdeutscher Blindenverband,* which was established in Brunswick in 1912, was the first national body of the blind people's movement in Germany. Its members were not blind individuals, but body corporates, that is, the organizations of the blind existing at the time.

3   Dr. Friedel Heister, Vice President of the German Federation of the Blind, 1950-1953; Dr. Fatima Shah, Past President of the International Federation of the Blind, 1974-1979; Mrs. Dorina Gouvea Nowill, Past President of the World Council for the Welfare of the Blind, 1979-1984; Dr. Salma Maqbool, Chairperson of the Committee on the Status of Blind Women, attached to the World Blind Union.

4   I do not attempt any technical definition here. I am using the term simply in the sense of "having no income of one's own." In many developing countries the social status of blind women is still very low. Most generally, the women do not receive any formal training which would help them to find a job and earn their living. Hence they depend on assistance provided by other people that is, husband or family. In many aspects, the status of blind women in the developing world resembles the social situation in which blind people found themselves for many centuries in Europe.

The ABCs of Disability

T. Christina F. Stummer
BRAZIL

THERE WAS A SHORT ceremony with no speeches, no special clothes, just a big black book we were to sign, and a formal handshake with the secretary. Not much of a graduation. But, in 1971, that showed a political attitude. The whole class had voted against the usual pomp and circumstance to protest against the dictatorship and its effects on student life in general. I heartily agreed with that, but personally, I had many reasons for a celebration.

While I waited for my turn, all the years that had led to this happy ending came to my memory. Delicious fruit juice, the wonderful taste of candy, my little table—all of it part of kindergarten. Those sensations, so alive after so many years, must have influenced my decision. I cannot really tell when I decided I wanted to be a teacher; learning, school, discoveries and life have always been so closely associated, they have been part of my life, just like my disability, my curiosity and my brown eyes.

In a family like mine—middle-class Brazilians—where my grandfather and his two sisters were teachers, as well as my grandmother, my mother and my aunt, not having an education was considered to be depriving oneself of many good things in life. Now I know how hard it must have been for my parents to try to convince people I belonged in a schoolroom, cerebral palsy or no cerebral palsy. Most of all, I suppose they were quite surprised to find out that people were not ready to accept me without putting up a fight first.

As I was only six, nobody had told me that the sisters who ran the big school for girls had refused to accept me—only many years later was I told that they thought I would not feel comfortable being the only disabled girl in that school. However, I was given my first chance by a friend of my parents who owned a school. And as he knew me well, he had all the reasons to think I would be at home with other kids. (How many other kids, I wonder, did not benefit from such favorable circumstances?)

Special class? No, thanks. Special treatment? No, thanks. There were a few inquisitive looks, and questions like, "Did you hurt your foot?"; "Can't you walk?"; "Not even if you try really hard?"; "How do you go pee if you can't walk by yourself?" Then everyone, including me, had a lot to do and so the novelty of a disabled classmate who needed help to walk soon wore out. Segregation only entered my vocabulary, or my life, in my early teens. Looking back, I think negative attitudes are a result of imitation and long training. Like an old song says, "You have to be carefully taught ..."

Strangely enough, most of the attitudinal barriers I came across were from professionals: teachers, nurses, doctors, politicians; in short, from people whose actions showed how unprepared they were for anyone or anything out of the ordinary. Even today, after forty years and some education campaigns, I still experience this feeling of "strangeness."

I remember how excited I was when my father got a much better job as a salesman and we moved back to Sao Paulo, the big city, where opportunities for medical treatment were the best Brazil could offer.

My brother went to a Catholic school and, as co-ed classes in the 1950s did not exist for the Fathers, I went to a public school. Not for too long, though. The principal wanted me to be tested. Why? I think her idea was that my brain was located in my legs and as I was not able to walk, my learning abilities could not be normal. Well, didn't I have cerebral palsy?

The psychologist, a very nice woman, seemed very embarrassed. The kinds of questions she asked me made me wonder if she was joking. After all, I was almost eight, my grandmother had taught me many beautiful words in French and I read a lot. Why then did she ask me all those silly things? Unable to go on with the game, and feeling very unhappy, I asked her, "Do you think I am stupid?" Quite surprised, she explained that she was assessing me for the school, that I was very intelligent and more than normal when it came to learning. No matter how Anna put it, I felt a bitter taste of humiliation in my mouth, and my family only made things harder for me when they did their best to make me forget the incident. I was told I was not going back to school. I never bothered to ask why; it was all too clear.

School or no school, learning was a joy and books were a continuous discovery, for words have always fascinated me. There was music on the radio, and there were games and places to "explore" with my brother and our cousin. If I was not wanted in that school, I could do without them, even though I missed a blue-eyed boy who used to teach me how to do my arithmetic.

The following year, I had an operation to straighten out my "ballerina feet," which made me stand on my toes. We moved back to Sorocaba, some one hundred kilometres away from Sao Paulo, and although I had to be carried up and down two enormous flights of stairs, going to school was no longer a problem. Accessibility? Both the word and the concept were unknown, I suppose. And, besides, why should they change anything for only one girl? A wheelchair would have been a great help but they belonged in hospitals and wheelchair users were "desperate cases" who stayed home or lived in hospitals.

Why should I be the only disabled person practically everywhere I went? This question would remain unanswered. Of course, there were others who, like me, could not walk without help. Where did they hide after they went to the doctor's, and why? This thought brings me back to the present, and for a moment, I come back to the graduation. Where are the disabled students? Certainly not among my sixty colleagues. That was, in part, understandable. Just imagine if my professors who had the "high and unique honor" (a Brazilian expression we used for the many times when they had to pick me up from the ground) had been made to help other students up those horrible stone steps?

To be fair, things have improved since a group of disabled students have been doing a fine, far-reaching job promoting awareness, talking to fellow students, and, most important of all, being there, showing that education and disability are not incompatible. Their activities are supported by the local Movement for the Rights of Disabled People. They are part of a lucky minority—in Brazil, tuition in state and federal universities is not paid for; admission depends on exams. What they need, like I needed, is moral support from their families and, in most cases, a fat budget—there is no government allowance—as well as lots of patience, for daily transportation remains a problem.

Now, much more than in those years, there is a general concern about education for young people. As for disabled children's parents, those who are uneducated do not always realize they should insist that their children be given the same opportunities as the general population. In this country, where inequality is the rule, opportunities are not given, they have to be fought for and conquered. Education for disabled people is a field that we must work in, with realistic goals: it should be regarded as one more door to be opened, not as a guarantee of success. In short, lack of education—particularly its most serious consequence, illiteracy—is one more disability, one that affects approximately twenty percent of our general population. In the specific case of disabled people, it adds up to a heavy burden—underemployment, more passivity. As for disabled women, education can put them in the fight for a bigger and better space in society.

"What is she doing here, a disabled woman? Why should she, of all people, take those special 'maturity' exams? Why not leave the place for the boys, who will either go to college or to work once they have their high school certificate?" My vivid imagination and old memories coming back? No, these are just old words that are still alive after more than twenty years. Maturity exams were a solution found by the authorities to solve a problem created by the great number of school drop-outs. People quit school to enter the workforce or because they lived in rural areas or simply because after some failures they decided to do something else; or they quit for health reasons, because of accidents or surgery, as the law at that time did not exempt one from attending class. Maturity exams meant full exams on the whole seven course program, taken in separate subjects. The final reward was a certificate, and the right to take entrance exams for college, just like everybody else.

Well, that "maturity" certificate meant a lot to me. It was the only way I could make up the time I had missed. It was an old story: some seven years before, we had learned that a foreign doctor was doing wonderful things with cerebral palsy patients. I decided to take the risks, which meant six major operations, six months in a plaster cast that came up to my armpits. I was ready to stand pain, but certainly not for what was to me, at sixteen, a final blow: after more than three kilos of legal papers (medical certificates and reports, school reports and the like) had travelled between Sao Paulo and our then-new capital "Brasilia," we found out that attendance in class was mandatory, and exceptions had to be submitted to the Ministry of Education. I had given up hope. Decisions were slow during the political turmoil. I swore never to set foot in a school again, even to attend other students' graduation ceremonies.

Despite my anger and frustration I spared books (in Portuguese, French, English and Spanish) and language courses—after all, they were not formal schools. As a result of my self-education, I found myself tutoring graduated high school and college students, and I would never be one of them!

Yet, when he left home for school every morning my brother looked like someone who was going to the dentist (or worse!). And my cousin seemed to enjoy school so much that he did all he could to fail every two years!

When I was taking my weekly physiotherapy exercises, I heard someone talking about "a very different psychiatrist" and that same day I stormed into her office, begging for help—one day before my twenty-second birthday. As I talked, I realized it was time to adopt a new strategy. Things were hard, nobody seemed to be aware of the barriers that made life so difficult for anyone with a "handicap." People would give money to help institutions, but they did not seem to realize they were helping people, living people with needs and dreams. Once I had tried to sell cosmetics door-to-door—a good way to use my crutches and make some money—only to hear things like: "Oh, dear, I don't need any makeup, but I'll be glad to give you some money ..."

As for the government, they preferred to ignore the problem—this was a comfortable position for them, because acknowledging disability issues would mean they would have to do something to make disabled people's lives less difficult. I believed, as I still do, that only educated people could contribute to changing this situation, to breaking this vicious circle: people with disabilities could not develop their potentials because they experienced a lack of supporting structures, and those structures would never be put in place unless people claimed them. This meant discussions, talking, taking opportunities to raise the subject, and showing doctors, authorities and the general public that we could speak for ourselves and that given the opportunities, we could, and would, be as creative and productive as anyone else.

So I decided to start all over again. In 1966, maturity exams were not popular. Only a few private courses dared squeeze all subjects taught in seven "normal" school years into a two-year program. Through a newspaper, I found the best of those "special" (and of course, very expensive) courses. Thank heaven one of the girls at the course kept me from falling head first down a steep flight of stairs, otherwise I might be dead (and buried under a pile of books). Once again, the question was, why bother about access for only one person?

Then, one day, there were *two* disabled female students, and classes were held on the ground floor for the rest of the year ... and then the time came ... the exams were there. Try to imagine how excited and nervous we all were, as we knew there would be questions covering four years of material. Many of us could not keep quiet in our places.

"This room is too noisy. You guys should be grateful for this opportunity to make up for the school years you missed." Echoing in that gloomy school room, those words were more than I could take. What did that man know about all these people? Many of them had studied by themselves, many of them came from other cities and needed the "maturity" certificate to keep their jobs. Whatever our personal motivation, we shouldn't be discriminated against. As noisily as I could, I picked up my crutches and left the room to get some fresh (and more friendly) air.

Back in the room and determined to show "them" that in spite of visible and invisible barriers nobody could stop me from getting what I wanted, I concentrated on the questions. Then I rushed outside to discuss the exams with the teachers. Knowing how much work and effort were involved, they were more nervous than they cared to show. They were aware of the quantity of dates and names we had had to absorb—in this kind of exam, quantity was the point. Things have changed since, and now students take one exam each semester for each subject. The program became more compact, in order to fit material into four years instead of the regular seven. One good thing: you do not have to travel from one city to another for reasons of timing (the exams were held only at certain times of the year)—and your own teachers correct your papers.

We were in the 1960s, a time when things kept happening, unexpectedly and fast, putting people in contact with a changing and often violent reality. For young Brazilians, 1966-67 meant living under extreme right-wing, repressive measures, in a sort of unclear witchhunt that was to become harder in the coming years. Unless you took all possible precautions you could be labelled a "leftist," and that meant serious trouble. The weirdest part of it all is that you did not really have to be involved in what was called "subversion," but you had to be able to prove you were not guilty of anything of the sort. A new equality of the sexes was created then: "subversives," men and women, were equal.

In a small town hotel, where I was getting ready for the last part of the "exam race" there was a sudden commotion: "Che Guevara is dead! They killed him somewhere in the jungle." Hiding my red eyes behind dark glasses, I joined the group taking a History test that morning and facing the "terror of Maths" in the afternoon. Loud voices attracted my attention and brought me back to reality. My mother was trying to explain that climbing up three flights of stairs would be too hard for me, and she was trying to talk the principal into allowing my class to use a room located on the ground floor (same size and same number of tables) for the exam. No way. Seeing me by the door, she winked at me and said, in her polite, quiet voice: "All right sir, my daughter will go upstairs, 'just like everyone else,' as you say, but if she has an accident, it is going to cost you your school ... and much more! Have a good day, sir!" And to me she said: "Start climbing up. I won't be able to help you."

When it came to disability issues, we could only count on other people's goodwill and common sense, which were subject to failure. Having determination also helped. This particular incident became one of the most effective advocacy campaigns in which I ever participated. Before I could take the first step, the order came: we would stay on the ground floor. I still strongly support having this attitude, and whenever discussing accessibility, this is my strategy: have a copy of the law with you, and show it. Other people might have never heard of it before. If this fails to convince, don't talk; act and let them feel that some of the absurd barriers faced by disabled people can and should be put down or minimized.

Ironically, my "maturity" certificate, the key to so many new challenges and opportunities, was signed by that reluctant man, who seemed totally unaware of the very existence of disabled people and of their issues. How many people like him were ready to take rights for privileges and how many fortunate ones, like me, had a member of the family or a friend to back them up?

As I remembered all that, while waiting for my turn to sign the black book that would entitle me to get my college diploma—my Bachelor of Arts in French and Portuguese/Brazilian Language and Literature—it was clear to me that I was a privileged person, in the sense that not many could get as far as I had. I also knew this knowledge, this feeling of achievement did not belong to me alone. Much of the credit went to those who had believed in me and had been able to look beyond the disability to see the woman, the student.

I wonder if all those mixed feelings could be seen on my face when my turn came and I asked that the book be brought to me. A privilege? No, all those memories had stirred many emotions and I felt very tired. As I signed, a warm and unexpected round of applause filled the room. A sign of sympathy? I can't say for sure, though I am certain none of my colleagues will be an obstacle for any disabled person they come across.

Later that same year, I got a scholarship to study in France. Thanks to a "travel now, pay later" plan, I had been to Europe before, and had noticed deep differences in attitudes towards disability issues. In England I saw for the first time the International Symbol of Access and wondered if that meant "No wheelchairs allowed" or "Wheelchair accessible." Being a disabled person in a developed country meant something quite different from what I had experienced. I did not have to wonder where other people like me were: they travelled, they were everywhere, they had organizations to fight for their rights and they participated more fully in everyday life. There was still a lot more to be done—but slowly and surely they were doing it. Take, for instance, the special transportation system. If you wanted to go to the University, you were picked up at the dorm by the *Groupement des Intellectuels Handicapés Physiques* (Group of Physically Disabled Intellectuals) and you could use their services to go to the bank and to do your shopping.

At present, we are trying to start a similar system here in Sao Paulo, but a part of the group does not agree with such a goal. They feel door-to-door transportation is for school children. Personally, I believe that transportation would allow many people with disabilities to have better chances for participation in society, as this would minimize their forced seclusion. Two of the important possibilities would be access to education and to the work market.

The more I participate in meetings and discussions, the more clearly I see two specific objectives have to be pursued: first, the elimination of all kinds of barriers (attitudinal, architectural, paternal and last but not least, personal barriers, by which I mean conformity). "If things are so difficult for the non-disabled, they are impossible for me," is a typical way of thinking; and, second, the participation of disabled persons in all fields. This is a gigantic task and all those who engage in it have a lot to learn. Sharing experiences may change opinions and help break century-old positions.

Being a member, as I have said, of the "lucky minority"—a disabled woman who has worked for one year in Canada with Disabled Peoples' International, and who has secured a permanent job as a teacher and also as an official translator—I feel free to say, "I have made it." This victory, if I may say so, is even more significant because it was achieved in a country where there is still a prevalent paternalism, as well as a great inequality of opportunities for women.

And I insist, education, either formal or informal, is not a magic key, nor a wonder drug that can give people defences against the various problems of underdevelopment and prejudice. Some doors may be hard to open, and some attitudes, such as the tendency to consider women as inferior beings, especially if they are disabled, are hard to change. My advice is, if these things cannot be done by a single person, try to do them in a group. If the saying, "Where there is a will there is a way" is applied to a group of people, there will be more ways, more options—and more people to benefit from them.

METAMORPHOSIS

Gem Wirszilas
CANADA

IT IS STRANGE HOW an ordinary event, on an ordinary day, can change your life. In a freak accident ten years ago, I broke my ankle and tore the ligaments in my foot. What appeared then to be a delay in my life was a complete change in lifestyle. It took five surgeries and seven years before I accepted myself as disabled. It was a life-altering process that affected me, my family and my friends.

It is difficult for an "outdoors" person who is an amateur naturalist, enjoys camping, and is a Girl Guide leader, to acknowledge that her life has changed forever. My dream of hiking the arduous West Coast Trail had to be replaced by going to a park with accessible trails. I am still involved with Girl Guides as an advisor, but now I camp in a lodge rather than in a tent. I treasure my contacts with nature and with the girls, but the focus of my life is the women with disabilities who have become my friends.

In 1987, my friend Eunice, who had been housebound with agoraphobia for eight years, decided to venture to a conference of women with disabilities. She asked me to go with her for moral support. It was at this conference that I fully realized and accepted that I was also disabled in body and in attitude— I had thought that disabled people were different than me. I began to see that I could use my energy be joining with DisAbled Women's Network (DAWN) women to improve their lives and thereby improve my own.

The concept of DAWN, the DisAbled Women's Network, was born in Canada's capital, Ottawa, in 1985. The federal government funded a meeting of seventeen women with various disabilities, from all regions of the country, to discuss disabled women's issues. They identified the following as the basic issues important to women with disabilities:

–access to the women's movement and to services
–employment
–sexuality
–parenting
–self-image and self-esteem
–violence and abuse

After this meeting, several groups that called themselves "DAWN" were formed in various provinces. DAWN Canada was formed in Winnipeg in 1987 to act as a liaison between individual groups across the country, and to lobby for all women with disabilities.

DAWN BC, the DisAbled Women's Network of British Columbia, was chartered in 1986 at a founding conference in Surrey, a suburb of Vancouver. Our goals are to improve the quality of the lives of women with disabilities and their families. DAWN BC is open to any women who considers herself disabled. We avoid issues, such as abortion, which would divide the membership. Naturally, members can hold and act on beliefs outside the group. We have over a hundred members networking with each other.

Every woman has a nugget of information or a contact that is useful to someone else. Since its inception four years ago, DAWN BC has formed an extensive library of self-help material. Our group is interconnected with groups concerned about advocacy for disabled persons, violence against women, employment, poverty, racism, access for disabled people, human rights, victim assistance, women's centres and transition houses.

Although we are unique voices, speaking from geographical diversity and differences in culture within BC, often isolated from each other, not only by mountainous geography, but by prevailing attitudes in the regions, we share a common goal to enrich our daily lives. We find the "able" in each newcomer, empowering one another. I have discovered that whatever a woman's disability is, we have commonalities which unite us.

Active members learn useful skills. For instance, DAWN BC promotes itself through radio programs produced by a collective of members, through newspaper articles and through a quarterly newsletter. The first DAWN conference I attended focused on starting a business. I have never started a business, but many of the things I learned have helped my family avoid mistakes in financial planning.

In the years since I joined, I have learned many things about the vast range of disabilities and needs. For instance, women—more often than men—are told that their hidden disabilities are psychosomatic. Our culture expects us to be able to control our bodies. Doctors often get angry with women whose diseases they cannot heal. This knowledge has given me more empathy toward others, and some insight into problems we have yet to surmount to gain equality.

The third DAWN conference theme was "Violence and the Disabled Woman." In North America, our culture sanctions a competitive struggle for riches and power, which leads to the abuse of the less able. Often these are abuses that poverty brings, such as not having enough money to pay for necessities or services. Sometimes the abuse is physical or sexual, victimizing someone who cannot defend herself effectively. So there is a need for emergency shelters (transition houses) for mobility-impaired people—places to think over options, and to let wounds heal with support and counselling. Women with disabilities are more likely to be victims of abuse, yet in this province no transition house is completely accessible to mobility-impaired women. DAWN BC is endeavouring to bring about change by lobbying the government and boards of transition houses.

Shortly after I joined DAWN in 1987, I was asked to sit on the board. I was hesitant, struggling with my new identity as a disabled person, but then I realized that so were others. In my second year, I took on the role of treasurer. In addition to my regular duties, I arranged and facilitated two "Anger Workshops." Writing a grant proposal to get funding, contacting women in need, and facilitating workshops were all new to me. I did not know what to expect of that first workshop, but after a shaky start, we voiced pain and disappointments, discovering links between us. We used techniques for diffusing anger, guided visualizations, music and candlelight to relieve tension. Everyone expressed pleasure in our time together, and in the sense of unity and strength that flowed between us.

Our 1989 conference on "Family Life" showed us that stigma

and isolation are destructive to disabled women. There are barriers in family life with a parent who is disabled, such as: not being able to fully participate in school and community activities due to physical inaccessibility; lack of understanding from others; added difficulties in everyday life such as getting dressed; frequent and profound fatigue due to chronic disability; uncertainties about our future; frustration with the medical community; and coping with being "different."

Children are welcome at any DAWN BC function. At last year's conference, there was a separate agenda for children which included role playing, dramatization and peer counselling. Children of mothers with disabilities have more responsibilities than their peers, with power they may not be able to handle. This can and does cause resentment, often directed towards the mother, which leads to feelings of guilt, acting out, and worse behaviour. We think that a program of drama, music and creative art can help children express themselves in a positive way. We do not pretend to be child psychologists, but we do know that healthy ways to play can increase feelings of self-worth and relieve tension. We are not able to deal with extreme dysfunction, but are prepared to recommend systems already developed for those who are seriously troubled.

It is hard to explain the bonding that has taken place between the young and older participants in DAWN events. Sometimes events are the only contact we have, but the warmth of friendship endures. I have friends all around the province who welcome me in their homes. We chat about common concerns and how problems have been solved.

Disability tends to isolate women who live outside the metropolitan Vancouver area. Distances between homes and towns separate women from each other. For instance, it is a drive of 143 kilometres from Terrace to the nearest town, Prince Rupert, without even a home in-between. Long winters and lack of accessible transportation keep women housebound for weeks at a time. This leads to depression. The phone could be a lifeline, but for some members, calling their neighbour is a toll charge: for example, a disabled woman in Spillimacheen, whose children go to school in Invermere twenty-eight kilometres away, and whose lifeline is the women's centre in Golden, twenty-eight kilometres in the opposite direction, cannot phone either place without a hefty charge.

In the next few years, we will tour more of the province, contacting women's centres, public health nurses, members and others who will help us reach more women with disabilities. We will present a two-day anger/assertiveness workshop, called "Take Time To Talk," to unite women in a way which we hope will lead to self-help groups. Our workshops teach participants techniques to diffuse anger, to increase self-esteem and to achieve emotional well-being. Funding for this eighteen-month project has come from the Department of Health and Welfare Canada.

Being a member of the board of DAWN BC, and participating in its growth and development, has enriched my life. There are many strengths and skills I now have that I only admired in others ten years ago. I often speak to the managers of restaurants and businesses about alterations to premises which would make them accessible to disabled consumers. Changes are often simple, such as altering the direction in which a door swings, but the problem is not apparent to able-bodied people. Since I took a course on assertiveness at our local college, my self-esteem has increased, and I can speak with confidence to small or large groups.

This is an exciting time for me to be a member of a group that is setting trends in the disabled people's movement. I am helping to make these changes happen. Many people still have medieval attitudes about disability. We must educate them by becoming visible and vocal.

Social change can be effected through political and social activism. For instance, a professor of philosophy, who is herself disabled, offered a course called "Women with Disabilities" at Simon Fraser University. I took this course and my concepts of disability have broadened. I have learned that women with disabilities are regarded as "not quite" women when it comes to sexuality, parenting, education, employment and social life. I am no longer willing to wait for changes to occur. The things I have learned as a woman with a disability, and as a member of DAWN BC, will be the tools I use to overcome stereotyping. They are the building blocks I use to improve community services and strengthen the ties that unite me with other women with disabilities, and they are the inspiration that will carry me forward.

DRAWING

zana
UNITED STATES

COMMON BARRIERS, JOINT SOLUTIONS
A Personal International Experience

Maria Cristina Mathiason
AUSTRIA

IN JULY 1987, MY husband and I moved to Vienna, Austria. When the airplane arrived at Vienna International Airport, my husband helped me down the steps. An ambulance belonging to the airport authority was waiting to drive me to customs and immigration. In spite of everything, we had arrived. This act was symbolic of how we, a United Nations family, had finally adjusted to my disability. After eleven years in New York, where I was barely able to leave my apartment, I could begin a new life, even though I was disabled. This is my story—what happened to me and what I learned in different cultures about being a disabled person.

I was not always disabled. I was born in Chile to a Bolivian father and a Chilean mother and I lived a normal life until after my second child and last child was born in 1969. I was twenty-six, and I began to have a terrible pain in my right wrist. The doctors diagnosed it as rheumatoid arthritis. This is a disease which strikes predominantly women, very often after young women experience childbirth. Sometimes it is not severe, but in my case it got progressively worse. The disease makes joints inflame and eventually renders them unusable. Its effects are permanent. By the time I was thirty-five I was severely disabled, unable to cope, take care of my children, do basic housework or meet my own basic needs.

When I began to become disabled, we were living in Seattle, Washington. My husband, an American, had completed an assignment with the United Nations in Venezuela as a rural development expert. We had met in Venezuela, where my family had moved after I had completed my baccalaureate studies. I was working as a secretary for a stockbroker, but I stopped working when our first child was born. My husband and I returned to the United States so that he could complete his doctorate, and after that he accepted a position teaching at the University of Washington. Even after the arthritis started, I worked as a volunteer to help foreign students adjust to the university, helped my husband do research and took courses at the university. We hoped to return to Third World countries to work on projects to help peasants and other poor people. This was his work when we met in Venezuela, and of course I shared his ambitions and was willing to follow him. But as my situation became worse, we began to face the fact that our life would have to be organized around my disability and it took a long time for my husband, our two sons and me to work this out.

I. ADAPTING TO DISABILITY IN DIFFERENT ENVIRONMENTS

A year after my arthritis started, my husband rejoined the United Nations in New York. We intended this to just be a temporary stop until we could obtain an assignment with the United Nations to live in a developing country. However, even this headquarters job meant that he had to go on frequent missions to developing countries. I continued my treatment and began to discover the problems of trying to care for small children in a big city with a disability that was growing in severity. One time when my husband was away in Brazil, I went to my doctor for my regular gold shot and then had a toxic reaction on the subway. The children were being taken care of by a Japanese friend whose husband, fortunately, was a doctor. I barely made it to the friend's house, where I collapsed.

After this, we decided that my husband would not be able to travel unless we had very well-organized arrangements to look after me. At the beginning, whenever he travelled I would usually stay with my parents. Other disabled friends also ask their parents for help, but our problem was that my parents lived in Venezuela. Sometimes we would hire a companion to stay with the children and me. Other times, there was no alternative but to travel with my husband. These arrangements were not really very satisfactory because they were expensive and worked only until the children entered school. Once they were in school, we could no longer take them out of school every time a mission appeared. However, since I was still able to walk and use my arms, I could shop and look after the children. Finally, so that we could all be in the field together, my husband accepted an assignment with the United Nations Development Program in Pakistan and in 1974 we moved to Islamabad.

PAKISTAN: BECOMING MORE SEVERELY DISABLED

While my arthritis was in remission, I could still do many normal things in Pakistan. I could drive a car, take care of the boys and accompany my husband to social events. After a year, however, I got food poisoning on a vacation in Sri Lanka and my arthritis flared tremendously. The weakness of health care in developing countries was clear: no doctors accurately diagnosed what was wrong. While a misdiagnosis could have occurred anywhere, in a developing country it was difficult to get second opinions, adequate laboratory work and the support services on which "scientific" medicine depends.

As I became more and more sick, the other problems of society in relation to my kind of disability became clear. Only men worked as cooks and housekeepers and I really didn't have anyone to look after me except the wife of our *chowkidar* (watchman) who, unfortunately, spoke no language I could understand. As this was a Muslim country, women did not work, so it was difficult to find someone to help me with bathing and the like. Moreover, our servants were very afraid that I was so sick that I might die and would pray at my bedroom door and cry! It was a shock for me and my family.

Disabled people were not very evident in Pakistan. The only ones I remember seeing were beggars, always men or children. I know that others existed, since my husband was involved with a UN project to improve an orthoprosthetic clinic which was mostly for disabled Pakistani war veterans. I do not remember ever seeing a disabled woman.

My condition became so severe that the doctors decided I would have to be evacuated to a place with better care. Unfortunately, as an international family, we had no home base to speak of and it was decided that I would go to my parents in Venezuela. In going from one developing country to another, I saw how little disability is understood. For eight months I was sent from doctor to doctor, since none in Venezuela wanted the case.

Seeing me sick and then having me go away for such a long time had very negative effects on the boys. My younger son seemed confused, felt guilty and did poorly at school. Having to take care of our sons alone made my husband more helpful and understanding of the double burden women face. My husband decided, as a result, to return to New York. We had a reunion in Venezuela and decided to try again to deal with both work and the arthritis.

NEW YORK: REPAIRING THE DAMAGE

When we returned to New York, I was severely disabled. I was no longer able to handle the boys because I was less active, in constant pain and simply unable to cope with their needs. It was very difficult for me to handle myself as my joints began to break and I needed constant care. We began to organize an environment which made it possible to cope. We moved into an apartment next to the boys' school and close to the United Nations. My husband's job still involved missions, and it always seemed that difficulties would arise whenever he travelled.

I also had to have frequent doctor's appointments. Since I could still walk, although not easily, I tried to go alone at first. But soon I found that taxis would not stop for me since I looked obviously ill, or if they did, they would not help me enter or leave. As I felt too insecure to continue going by myself, my husband or someone else would have to accompany me to all appointments and I grew increasingly more dependent.

To correct the damage done by the disease, I began a long series of surgeries which disturbed the boys as I had to leave them while I was in the hospital. We managed to cope through two knee and hip replacements, a neck fusion and ten hand surgeries from 1977 through 1987. We also became dependent on having a housekeeper, a full-time nurse for a year-and-a-half, nurse's aides, therapists, and a psychiatrist who worked with the whole family. At the time it did not bother me, as I needed the attention of each of them and in any case, felt helpless without them. With time I started not to need all of them. We would not have been able to cope financially if the United Nations had not had an excellent health insurance plan. Even so, it was expensive and we gave up most luxuries.

After trying to travel on business for no longer than two weeks, my husband finally transferred to a post which required no travel at all. He was not happy with this, but we discovered that there was no alternative, especially while the boys were teenagers. Raising boys in New York with a handicap was my biggest problem. I lacked the ability to keep firm control over them as I could not chase after them, and during the extended periods of surgery and recovery, it was difficult to supervise them and give them the attention they needed. Peer pressure was very strong on all of my children's friends, but the ones with stricter supervision seemed to resist it better. My husband was at work most of the day and had to give primary attention to me at home. Moreover, as an international family, we had no relatives in the city at all. We depended on ourselves and occasionally on friends. Fortunately, United Nations people understood my situation since most of them were also displaced in one way or another. We tended to develop a form of surrogate family relationship, where we helped each other whenever the need arose.

VIENNA: REBUILDING A NORMAL LIFE

After eleven years recovering from our last field assignment, I finally went into remission, the boys graduated from high school and my husband and I decided that it was time to work in the field again. I tested my ability to travel by accompanying my husband on missions to Jamaica and Bolivia in 1985. Both Jamaica and Bolivia were difficult for disabled persons since no buildings were designed to be accessible and transportation for disabled persons was almost non-existent. But I was able to cope. Having more money relative to the poverty of the country was important, I discovered. We could afford taxis and wheelchairs; most people there could not. Most disabled people could not even leave the house. Crowded, chaotic public transportation is difficult for disabled people to use. In Bolivia, wheelchairs are not readily available. The airport in La Paz had only one wheelchair and it took an hour to find it. Also, La Paz is an old city that has not been designed to make places more accessible. This is because the city is in a valley and streets are hilly, usually cobblestone, with many stairs. The country is very poor and it is difficult to change these conditions quickly.

But, more importantly, disabilities are considered abnormal and perhaps even a matter of shame. With me people were very helpful, but I think my husband's position helped because United Nations officials are given a certain status. I went with him to meetings and on field trips, since there was no alternative. I began to learn his work. I helped him on a personal research project where I classified resolutions of the United Nations General Assembly by content.

My husband had an opportunity to apply for a post in the United Nations Office at Vienna, at the Branch for the Advancement of Women. We visited Vienna for a meeting in the middle of winter and discovered that the Austrian government had made a great effort to make the city accessible to handicapped people. Ramps, special parking facilities, special access to theatres and museums, elevators, all help disabled people to be more mobile. Moreover, disabled people pay reduced fares and tariffs for public services.

My husband won the post and we moved. We have found an apartment which is small, but completely accessible, and only minutes away from my husband's office. His colleagues help by taking me places when my husband is not available, and I am welcome in the office and am considered a part of their group. The program of advancement for women is very ambitious and there is only a small staff to work on it, so any help is welcome. I help translate material from English to Spanish and vice versa.

More importantly, I have been able to use the knowledge of the United Nations which I acquired over twenty years of living within it to help disabled people. I am the Vienna representative of Disabled Peoples' International (DPI) and thus can act as a bridge between the United Nations and disabled people everywhere. For the first time in years I feel that I can do something useful again. I represent DPI to the United Nations Office at Vienna and cover all of the social aspects related to people with disabilities, such as aging, the advancement of women, and the family. I try to make sure that the UN pays attention to training both disabled and non-disabled people to help people with disabilities, to educate the public, and to establish humane policies.

II. INTERNATIONAL LIVING: SOME LESSONS

BEING A WOMAN IS A HANDICAP

In most countries being a woman is in itself a handicap. Although there has been much progress in the last few years, women still have a long way to go before they are treated equally. The problem is not legal, since many countries have laws that prohibit discrimination. Rather, the problem is in the customs of countries and attitudes of both men and women towards women. This was most visible to me in Pakistan, where women are not often seen and have less opportunities. In South America the problem is the *machismo* which says that women must be objects that run the house, serve the man and the children and are physically perfect. When these attitudes are added to those about disabled persons, they are a double handicap.

One of the important ways to change attitudes and customs is to encourage real partnership between husband and wife. As long as the husband is expected to work outside and relax at home, the burden of managing the household falls on the woman. It is a burden which should be shared. In my case, my husband was willing to share even before I became disabled. When I did become disabled, sharing was necessary to survive. Curiously, although my disability would have prevented any such activity, it would have been physically less taxing for me to work at an office job than to do all of the housework. I wonder how many other disabled women experience the same situation.

In societies where a woman's worth is measured only in terms of the home, I can see how disabled women are not well-regarded when they are not able to contribute to the work of the home.

COMMUNICATING

Moving from one country to another has dramatized for me the problems of international communication. Language differences are particularly difficult for disabled people since we depend a lot on our ability to ask people for help. It doesn't matter whether the language is German, Punjabi or Quechua: if you can't speak it, life can be very difficult. But I have also learned that if you try, people will understand and will help. There is a universal language of compassion.

It is sometimes more difficult to learn that you have to ask for help. This is particularly important in countries where we cannot cope by ourselves. To be able to reach out to a stranger costs a lot because of culture and language. For example, on a recent trip to Yugoslavia and Greece I noticed a large difference between countries. In Yugoslavia, where there is little accessibility for wheelchairs, wherever we stopped people would surround us and stare as though we came from outer space. No one would volunteer to help carry the wheelchair. In contrast, in Greece, people would help without being asked and saw me as a normal, active person. I have learned to try to reach people by greeting them in a friendly way. Some respond positively and others seem to ignore my existence. But I have never seen a rejection, if I try hard enough anywhere we have been.

It is also a matter of communicating about disabled people's rights. When I travelled on buses in New York, I had to insist that non-disabled people give up the seats that were reserved for disabled persons. Also, in New York one evening I saw a bus driver refuse to board a disabled person in a wheelchair because it was too inconvenient for him. A companion of the disabled person stood in front of the bus and would not move until the bus driver boarded the wheelchair user. We have to learn to be assertive, particularly about public services, just to function like everyone else.

SERVICES AND FAMILIES

In some respects it is easier to be disabled in a developed country than in a developing one. I have lived in both. In developing countries, there are fewer services for disabled persons. Governments think that because of the endemic poverty, providing accessible buildings and transportation, as well as education and training is too expensive. They have not learned that with a small investment disabled people can help other disabled people to become more active, and younger disabled persons can be educated to grow up in a society where there are fewer barriers.

Disabled persons, given a chance, can use their intelligence and skill for the benefit of themselves and society.

My husband told me about a rehabilitation project in Pakistan where just a little training and a new carving machine made it possible to produce inexpensive artificial limbs that could make disabled people functional again. Also, the cost of making buildings accessible is really not high and can be done with little additional cost, especially if it is done in the design stage.

One real problem connected with poverty in the developing world is that it makes people do very little for disabled people. They hide disabled family members, especially women, because they are ashamed of them. If people have learning disabilities they are not sent to school. If they have a physical disability they are kept in bed. In developing countries there is a belief that a person is disabled because he/she is cursed or brings bad luck. Thus, the family does not want these members to be seen in public, unless the disability was obviously the result of an accident. What is ironic is that if opportunities and incentives were provided, the disabled people could contribute. Or the disabled person could make his or her own alternatives. A disabled person can gain self-esteem by receiving training from an early stage. They need to be shown that they are intelligent and capable of thinking like any non-disabled person. Disabled people also have to learn to be a little aggressive and fight for their rights: we have to make ourselves heard!

There is a curious paradox in the extended family, wherever it is found. I noted that I have not really been able to fall back on my family for support because we have usually lived far away from them. Most disabled people survive because they are taken care of by their families. This is often seen as a reason why social services should not be provided by the government or by the community: families do a better job, say the critics of public involvement in support activities. Indeed, when I visited my father's extended family in Bolivia, I was well taken care of by my uncles, aunts, cousins and their families. But I thought that the care was frequently suffocating. They wouldn't let me do anything. They treated me as though I was helpless. It was an unpleasant feeling, since I can think, make my own decisions and, even if I am not very active, I can handle myself with some assistance, talk, ask for what I need. I am not a vegetable nor something strange.

I think the "overcare" that families often give is one reason why I seldom saw disabled people in public in developing countries. They were kept at home because there they could be attended and supervised more closely. Families often thought that disabled persons were not capable of coping with the outside world because of their disability. It was easier that way. Paradoxically, I think that I have been able to emerge because I didn't have too much of that kind of help.

I appreciate the services in Europe for disabled people. I think that these countries have come to terms with disability. They have decided that disabled people are citizens too, and that we can and should be an equal part of society. In my neighbourhood in Vienna, I see many disabled veterans of World War II, for whom services have been provided. There are also many older people. The public housing development next door, like all public housing in the district, has just installed elevators. The City of Vienna published a book on accessibility to all public buildings for disabled people. On a recent trip through the Federal Republic of Germany, I was happy to see that facilities for disabled people were clearly marked and available at almost all rest stops along the highways. In Norway, I saw some pedestrian traffic lights that make sounds when it is safe for pedestrians to cross, so that blind people can cross safely. I observed that people there did not even seem to notice disabled people—we were considered a part of the population.

Things are not perfect, however. In Vienna there are few homes that we can visit easily, since there are usually stairs, even to reach the elevators. And people who are not disabled still park in parking spaces reserved for disabled people. But at least there is the beginning of public consciousness.

My husband and I have learned by experience that acquiring services in a developed country tends to cost a lot. Ironically, poor disabled people sometimes have easier access to services than do the middle class. In New York, I had a disabled friend who was poor. The city provided food stamps, rent supplements, therapy and other services which she needed and some of which we could not have afforded for ourselves. Another time, I was sent by one of my doctors to see about vocational rehabilitation. I wanted to have the option of returning to work if anything happened to my husband. I found out that I did not qualify because my husband's income was too high. And so I could not be trained, even though it would have equipped me to be a wage earner. Yet I know that if we had been poor, I probably would not have learned about the service in the first place. And in a developing country the service probably would not exist. The idea that a disabled woman can have a career is becoming more accepted, but is no more easy to achieve in reality, and really depends on public services.

COMMON BARRIERS, JOINT SOLUTIONS

The barriers all disabled women encounter, whether in developed or developing countries, mean that we have more in common than we have differences. We can and should be united in struggling internationally for both the rights of disabled persons and of women. The nature of my disability kept me somewhat isolated, but by living in different cultures and environments I think I have gained some insights into the universal situation of disabled persons. In Vienna, I am able to meet with other disabled persons and exchange ideas. The United Nations has a Disabled Persons Unit in which there are two disabled persons working, and I belong to the NGO Committee on Disability, on which there are other persons with disabilities. Our problems have a common nature, as does our own misunderstanding of our capacities.

I have learned that it is important to have allies. I have had a friend and companion in my husband. Because of his work and mine, we now have even a more common goal: the struggle for disabled women. Thinking that disabled women are less able to do things and we are not complete persons, people tend to ignore us and not include us in their discussions. But over the last few years, I have learned to make people hear my voice, and they cannot ignore me.

GROWING UP
Creating a Movement Together

Judy Heumann
UNITED STATES

THOSE OF US WHO have had disabilities at different life stages have different concerns about risk taking and responsibilities. I contracted polio when I was one-and-a-half years old in 1949, in Brooklyn, New York. Because I was disabled early in life, I had to face the possibility of being told that I have to fit into a system which frequently does not want me to be there.

A few years ago, in the 1950s, segregated school systems, or no school systems at all, for disabled people were very common. When it was time for me to go to school, my mother, an immigrant from Europe, took me to the local public school in New York and was informed by the principal that I was a fire hazard and therefore could not go to that school.

My father and mother went through all the worries and trepidation that other parents go through, knowing that it was important for me to get an education, but not knowing how to deal with a system which operates for seven million people.

My parents were the strongest role models in my formative years because they did not accept the system's statement that I could not go to school. For about four years I had a teacher who came to my house for an hour-and-a-half twice a week. This was called "Home Instruction" and was paid for by the city schools. I guess this meant that the system worked on the assumption that I would not do very much with education, so they just threw me a bone.

My mother was searching for special classes in Brooklyn, but did not find anything satisfactory. She also tried to get me into *Usheba* (a Jewish school). She took me to the school and the principal informed her that he would love to take me but could not because I did not speak enough Hebrew. My mother spent 200 dollars on tutoring by a woman from Israel whose first language was Hebrew. I remember how disappointed we all were when my mother called up the principal to tell him that I could probably speak better Hebrew than anybody else in kindergarten and it turned out that the principal had never wanted me in the program. He had used the mastery of Hebrew as a way of keeping me out, never suspecting that my mother would take him up on this excuse. At that time we had no laws which protected you against discrimination on the basis of disability. So we continued our search for a special program.

Finally in the middle of fourth grade, I got into "Health Conservation 21." We never understood what that name was supposed to mean. Acceptance into this program was a major achievement. I was the first polio student. All the other kids had cerebral palsy. When my friend, Freda, was accepted she was the first kid with muscular dystrophy.

We were housed in the basement of the school. In my class there were kids as old as twenty-one years of age. Age appropriateness was not relevant if you happened to be disabled. Academics were not given a high priority either. In this program the parents had to come in as part of the screening process. One advantage of the ruling that parents had to provide attendant care was that they saw what was not being taught in the classroom. I'd ride the bus for two hours in the morning and two in the evening—but when I'd get to school there was no hard learning. We'd have lunch, then an hour rest period—I guess they thought that we'd been so active we needed this rest. In between rests, we were taken out for physical therapy and speech therapy. Every once in a while some academics were taught, but nothing to strain the brain very much. I remember Miss Cutter (I will never forget her name) was teaching us how to make pizza. I guess that was the last straw for my mother. She got the teacher transferred to another school. My mother had learned about power and had become friends with the assistant principal. This was the first time I witnessed power-brokering!

However, my first real experience meeting other disabled people occurred in the school. I remember the feeling of relief when I was finally able to talk to other disabled people, who confirmed that my experiences as a disabled person were all too real. Yes, people did stare when I went down the street. Yes, it was true, many people around me felt that it was a tragedy that I had a disability, and yes, these experiences had an effect on me. As a group of disabled peers we were sometimes able to laugh at those experiences. We were able to acknowledge our experiences and organize around them.

I remember that one of the most powerful experiences for me was when I realized that it was fine for a group of us with visible disabilities to go into the street together. We had once been embarrassed to go down the street. But, now, finally, we were willing to risk the exposure. I had thought that if I went down the street by myself people wouldn't notice my wheelchair.

I did not fully realize, until I was about eight-and-a-half or nine years old, that people saw that I had a disability. I was relieved when a Swedish study which came out a few years ago showed that the age when disabled children realize they have a disability is between the ages of eight and ten. I was eight-and-a-half when a kid came up to me on the street and asked what was the matter with me. I started to cry because I realized that kids noticed my wheelchair.

In school we talked to each other about situations such as, "What would you do if you were going down the street and somebody started staring at you?" We decided that we would turn around and say, "Take a picture, it lasts longer." I remember the first time we said this to somebody, who thought we had not noticed him staring. We didn't notice his reaction because we were laughing so hard. It was school experiences like these that made me realize that together with other disabled people we could assume power.

We were also learning at a very early age that if you had a speech difficulty or were mentally handicapped it was unlikely that you would successfully make it through the system. You could already see that happening in the "Health Conservation 21" unit: those of us with parents who were strong advocates and who had a vision for us were the ones who were going to achieve. Parents with vision had adult disabled role models, such as Franklin D. Roosevelt (a former President of the US), who was disabled as a result of polio. But for the parents of mentally handicapped and multiply-disabled kids there were not adult role models to follow. These kids would not graduate from school and obtain employment.

The visionary parents, including mine, were successful in raising our educational level to that of our non-disabled, ten-, eleven- and twelve-year-old peers. We started to set goals for ourselves and this was fundamentally important for me.

We learned that we had to believe in ourselves, because the system around us was not set up to help us succeed. If anything, it was set up to help us fail. The teachers did almost everything possible to allow the failure syndrome to become reality. When I graduated from the eighth grade I was the first student from those classes to ever go on to high school. Though the classes had been going on for many years, most of the students had been sent to sheltered workshops. And it was very difficult for these students to ever move beyond the workshops. This was a message which many of us took to heart because we had very strong negative feelings about sheltered workshops. Low self-esteem was, and is, being reinforced there through people being segregated, performing menial tasks and earning substandard wages.

We also realized very early on that the people working with us—the "professionals"—were not disabled, and we realized that they did not have a strong vested interest in whether or not we made it in life. The teachers never talked about our futures. They never said, "If you want to get a job you have to work hard in school." They got their paycheck and went home.

In 1969, I graduated from college and decided to become a teacher. At that time there were no people in wheelchairs who were teachers in New York City. I had known that when I started to go to college. In my third year I called the American Civil Liberties Association, an organization set up to assist person whose civil liberties have been violated. I told them I wanted to become a teacher, but needed to know what I should do since I was in a wheelchair. The response was that I should go to school and take the courses I needed. If I had any problems I was to call the organization.

I did not communicate my plans to the State Vocational Rehabilitation (which was a fund set up by the government to pay most of a disabled person's education, with the goal of employment), because they would not have granted me the money to become a teacher. Therefore, the options for support by Vocational Rehabilitation at that time were extremely limited—speech therapy or social work were fields that disabled women were strongly encouraged to pursue. So I majored in speech therapy, as did most of the other disabled women going to college at that time.

When you graduate from university in New York, you have to take a series of examinations—oral, written and medical—if you wanted to teach. I passed the written and oral exams, but I failed the medical examination. It was not that I had a contagious disease. When I met the doctor for my examination, she said that she had never seen or examined anybody like me. I replied, "If you fail me, I am going to sue you." I was young and had no negotiating skills. I would not say it the same way today, but it would not have made any difference. She had made up her mind about a person in a wheelchair and she failed me. That meant that I did not receive my teaching credentials.

Out of this incident a great movement grew up in New York. A friend of mine, who was disabled and had majored in journalism, convinced an established writer to do an article in the *New York Times* about my situation. This article spurred an editorial the next day in the *Times*: "Heumann vs. Board of Education." For a year, articles about this act of discrimination and other disability topics appeared in newspapers, and on TV and radio throughout the United States.

In the end, I sued the Board of Education in New York. We settled out of court and the decision was made in my favour. The judge in the case was the first black woman ever appointed to a federal district court in the US. She understood discrimination herself.

In 1970, I received my teaching credentials. I eventually taught for three years in New York City schools. But getting that first job was difficult because no one wanted to hire me. There was another series of articles in the newspaper about this problem, and, in the end, the principal of the school I had attended hired me. I taught non-disabled children in my first year, at the elementary level. Then I taught disabled children for two years.

Around this time, a friend and I decided that we were going to use my job discrimination issue to start an organization. We were getting hundreds of letters and phone calls from both disabled and non-disabled people; we were often stopped on the street and we were asked to do many TV and radio interviews.

We were neophytes, but we learned quickly that there were many problems in the world and that it was not just a few of us who thought these problems existed. There were many disabled people who wanted to take control of their lives. Many disabled people were very angry about the fact that traditional service organizations for them were not run by disabled people.

The goals of traditional service organizations did not reflect how we wanted to shape our lives. So we began to speak out about these problems. If you believe you have nothing to lose, which we did, you can do almost anything—and we did almost anything. We worked on issues regarding transportation and education, and we started to build coalitions among disabled groups. Parents became involved and we started working with groups which provided services to mentally retarded persons. At that time a huge scandal was uncovered regarding a state school for the mentally retarded, called Willowbrook. We became involved with the organization that had exposed the situation. And our belief that we had nothing to lose made us more combative, and many things began to change slowly.

I think that the shell we had built around us as disabled people had also segregated us from society. We were basically ashamed of who we were. We also knew that if we could not speak out about what was important to us very little was going to change. It became apparent to us that we had to *make* changes occur. The organization we founded as a result of my legal suit, "Disabled in Action," still exists in New York, Maryland and Philadelphia, and many of us are proud of our involvement in setting it up. We told people that the goals of service organizations were not what we wanted in our lives. There were no disabled persons on the boards of those organizations and no disabled persons had jobs there. In the 1970s, Disabled in Action tackled issues like transportation and housing, and launched demonstrations.

One of the first major activities of Disabled in Action was a demonstration against President Nixon's veto of the 1972 Rehabilitation Act. The Rehabilitation Act was a symbol for disabled people because it contained provisions for education, independent living, accessibility and anti-discrimination. The veto was a rejection of the wishes of our Congress of representatives. In our protest we shut down the President's re-election campaign headquarters in 1972 in New York City. We organized about fifty disabled people to come to this demonstration.

In New York there were hardly any private transportation systems and few of us had cars. So we went begging, and borrowing just to get transportation to go to the demonstration. We did not exactly know what we were going to do, but we decided to go to the Federal Building.

The Federal Building is on an island in the East River and there is nothing much around it. There were few people around and little traffic. But we finally found the building and eventually everyone knew we were there.

We had brought a coffin with us, and we talked about how the US Government was trying to kill disabled people. A representative from the Federal Building told us that were not allowed to be there and that he would call the police if we did not leave. When the police arrived they asked who was responsible for this demonstration. Everybody said that I was.

After a while we decided to move to the Nixon re-election headquarters on Madison Avenue, one of the big thoroughfares in Manhattan. At 4:40 pm, at rush hour, we stalled traffic for about forty minutes and we gained some press attention.

Finally, the day before the election, we organized another demonstration, and this time we brought two disabled Vietnam War veterans with us, who got a lot of press coverage in those days. Most of the New York press corps was there. We had a demonstration on Times Square and walked against traffic on Madison Avenue to the Nixon re-election headquarters. We wanted a public debate with President Nixon about why he had vetoed the Rehabilitation Act.

Unfortunately, a public debate was not called, but the experience gave us an incredible sense of power. We handed out thousands of flyers on the street explaining the impact of the veto of the Rehabilitation Act. The following year, the demonstrations continued full strength with a march and candlelight vigil in

Washington DC, and we also lobbied in the federal Congress. This time, the law was passed and it included the first civil rights legislation for disabled people in Section 504, comparable to the legislation for people of colour and women.

In 1973, I attended graduate school in Berkeley, California. I also worked with a group called the Centre for Independent Living (CIL). I found it a powerful experience to see severely disabled people live independently in Berkeley, largely as a result of the CIL. I had really been afraid to leave New York where I had a whole network of friends and relatives helping me, since there was no government paid attendant system (for personal care). I did not have my own van in New York and so I basically depended on enlisting help from others to get things done. I became a manipulator very early in my life and I think that is a prerequisite for anybody who is disabled. I learned to get as much as I could out of society.

The disabled people in Berkeley seemed to do things differently than we had done in New York. They were dissatisfied with the system, they felt that the professionally-run organizations were not meeting their needs. Disabled people were unemployed and disabled people were not board members of service organizations. The disabled people were afraid of going back to the institutions that they had just left. Their organization combined a strong militant advocacy with support services which were not designed to assume the responsibility of government or other non-profit organizations.

The fundamental principle of the organization was that it had to be controlled by disabled individuals. Paid attendant services had to be controlled by disabled people. People could work for the integration of disabled individuals into society, but on disabled people's terms. They wanted to be accepted for what they were—persons with disabilities. Integration for me means having pride, and thus being able to tell people what I need to integrate within an organization and into the community and society as a whole.

I am not ashamed of my need to have a group of disabled friends I can go back to regularly. We are willing to support each other. That is what independent living means to me. The Centre for Independent Living, and the more than 150 other independent living programs in the US, are places for disabled people to come for basic assistance in housing, attendant services etc. But, most importantly, centres are a powerful voice for integration and equality in our communities.

I gained valuable experiences during those years. I was on the CIL Board of Directors. I also did my Master's program internship in public health at a Senator's office in Washington and learned how laws and regulations come about. Back in Berkeley I worked as Chief Deputy Director of the Centre for Independent Living and did program development serving disabled persons aged twenty and over. At first we were mostly serving people with physical disabilities and people who were blind. Over the years, services were developed for people who were mentally disabled, people who were deaf and people with multiple disabilities.

With the array of new services, the Centre for Independent Living became more diversified and more powerful. Disabled communities began to push hard for change. The concept that we had nothing to lose and everything to gain became stronger and stronger, and more and more changes occurred. Disabled people and some professionals from all over the United States and other countries started to come to Berkeley to voice their concerns and to learn first-hand how severely disabled people had changed their lives.

An important milestone in the development of independent living centres was federal legislation which provided program money within the Rehabilitation Act. The money was a paltry twenty-two million dollars, but it enabled Independent Living Centres to be established throughout the United States. Most of the Centres strongly support the philosophy of control by disabled people. Their core services include information and referral, and attendant care services. (There is no national attendant service in the US. Provision of attendant services is left to the discretion of the different states.) The disabled person hires, fires and trains the attendant but the Centre does the first screening. Thus, disabled persons have control over who they would like to provide their attendant care, and over how it is done.

Peer support is a fundamental part of Independent Living Centres—disabled people working with other disabled people in a peer-counselling relationship. It helps disabled people to realize that other people have been through the same experiences and that together they can work on getting on with life.

Some of the Centres provide job placement services and provide services for a wide range of disability groups. The Berkeley Centre now serves people with all types of disabilities. The fundamental goal of the Centre is to open its doors to all people who want to participate and to create access for disabled people to the benefits of society. The independent living movement subscribes to the philosophy that disabled people must have respect for themselves, that they know what is right for them, that they must have the ability to say "no" to somebody, that they can develop the ability to turn power around and manage it themselves.

To me independent living is: power, self-respect, the belief that we can make a difference, and the ability to make that difference through an international alliance of all disabled people. Today we see the independent living movement flourishing throughout the world in countries such as Canada, Germany, Sweden, Italy, Mexico, Nicaragua and Japan. We are disabled people articulating our needs and fighting for the right to be equal members of our communities. We have so much to accomplish, but we can be proud of the changes we have been initiating throughout the world. We are overcoming, today.

WE'LL DECIDE WHAT IS ...

Lesley Hall
AUSTRALIA

MARCH 8, 1981, IN MELBOURNE, Australia, a group of women met in the park. They held a banner that read: "We'll decide what is beautiful." On International Women's Day, for the first time, women with disabilities had come together, stood together, marched together. Another woman stood there too, not with the group, but disabled. She was invited to join the others and so began in Melbourne the first collective of disabled women.

I wasn't there. I was in Canberra, the national capital, attending a conference on employment, my first conference as disability rights activist. For the previous ten years I had been a feminist. I had also felt my oppression as a disabled person. There were plenty of things to be angry about. But I had thought I was alone. I had no contact with other disabled people who were organizing for their rights.

I didn't know of the existence of self-help groups, let alone the work they were doing. I was ecstatic when Yooralla (the institution for disabled people I had been in for a number of years) had dropped its annual telethon. But I did not know that it was disabled people who had made them do it.

I loathed and hated that telethon. I hated it when I was at Yooralla as the cameras, celebrities, and charity do-gooders came out each year, patronizing us, coming near only when the cameras rolled. I hated it, years after, as they continued to use stolen shots of my body. Every year the world where I lived saw visions of me that I had no part in making, had given no permission for them to take or continue showing, and that presented me only as an object for pity.

I was angry at this theft and at the continuous discrimination I was confronting because of my disability. I was angry about my forced institutionalization as a child and about the botched up medical treatment which the doctors called surgery. I was angry at the hype surrounding the coming International Year of Disabled Persons.

Then one night, at a party, I met another disabled person. We talked, he gave me things to read and I got involved in disability politics. I found myself in Canberra at a conference.

On the third day, one of the women in Canberra returned to Melbourne. She was going back for International Women's Day (IWD) and I should come too, she told me. I thought she was odd—it just another IWD. I preferred to stay in Canberra where I was learning new things.

So I didn't go back and I missed that International Women's Day. I missed the rally and I missed the public meeting for disabled women. But I did get involved.

We called ourselves the Disabled Feminist Collective. Some of us came from the Women's Liberation Movement, some from disability rights groups, and some had never been politically active before. But we came together and we talked.

We met over drinks in a pub, or at dinner in someone's house. We drank wine, we relaxed, and we talked. We told each other things we had never let go before. We exposed our pain, our fears, our vulnerabilities. We spoke of our bodies and our attitudes towards them.

We realized that we all had very low self-esteem. We had internalized too much to really like ourselves, to enjoy our body image. We spoke of trying to hide our disabilities, of proving we were "normal," and of the difficulties we had in forming relationships. We saw the similarities in our experiences.

For those first few meetings, we kept talking. Then we decided to act. We reclaimed our bodies. We ran a campaign around beauty quests (or pageants), gave out leaflets at marches, organized demonstrations, wrote to politicians, held public meetings. We felt strong in what we were doing. We broadened our campaign to include feminists without disabilities and a new group, the "Anti Miss Victoria Quest Working Party", evolved.

We left the issue of beauty quests with this newly-formed collective, and as the Women with Disabilities Feminist Collective we lobbied for other things. We took on the sexism within the disability rights movement and asserted our rights as women. We took on the Women's Liberation Movement and brought up the issue of disability. We were successful in getting the new women's building made (reasonably) accessible. We put out newsletters and started gathering any information we could find on women and disability. And we decided to write a book.

Six years later that book was finally published. We called it *Women and Disability—an Issue*. Many of the articles had been written when we originally conceived the idea. But when the book came out they were just as vibrant as the day they were first put to paper.

Some people had this to say:

"I found it painful and confronting to read, and needed the shakeup to remind me that many of the issues are still there, even with the victories we have chalked up."

"... a nice blend of the personal and political."

"Although you know these things happen, the articles made it real all over again."

"The issues you've raised affect us all and you've made me realize how often I still buy into all those conditionings."

The collective was very pleased with our final effort. It had been a real stop-and-start job. But we persevered. Putting the final touches on the book required enormous willpower for some of us and we were all looking forward to seeing the end of it. It's been such a thrill seeing our thoughts, and the thoughts of other disabled women, in print, that we now talk, jokingly, of doing another one.

The collective today is focused on the book's distribution. We are sending it throughout Australia and we received a grant to take it to women in institutions.

Our other activities have largely ceased, although the issue of beauty quests is still being fought by the "Stop All Beauty Quests Collective." When we're angry enough, we organize letter campaigns.

Most of the members of the original collective are no longer part of it. Personal support and consciousness-raising can only continue for a certain time. Once individuals feel stronger, they don't need the collective any more. And this is a good thing. It shows that the group is successful in achieving some of its aims.

Being disabled and female united us for a time. But the

differences among us, differences of class and race, were also bound to take their toll. Some of the women in the collective have moved on to other things. They have made personal choices to get jobs in government and the bureaucracy. Other women have continued to lobby and fight for the rights of disabled women from a self-help perspective.

Groups such as the "Women with Disabilities Feminist Collective" have only limited lifetimes. At one stage in our lives it was important for us to come together, to share our experiences, to fight for change. I am sure we were all strengthened in the process. But it is important also to let go, to create the space for new women to come together, and decide what *is*.

SELECTED BIBLIOGRAPHY

Baker, David, "Wrongful Sterilization", *Phoenix Rising: The Outspoken Voice of Psychiatric Inmates* 1 (Winter 1981):32-34.

Blumberg, Lisa, " '...For Who Among Us Has Not Spilled Ketchup?' " *Rehabilitation Gazette* 27 (1986):4-6.

Boylan, Esther. *Women and Disability*. London and New Jersey: Zed Books, Ltd., 1991.

Browne, Susan E., Debra Connors and Nanci Stern (eds). *With the Power of Each Breath: A Disabled Women's Anthology*. Pittsburgh: Cleis Press, 1986.

Burstow, Bonnie and Don Weitz (eds). *Shrink Resistant: the struggle against psychiatry in Canada*. Vancouver: New Star Books, 1988.

Campling, Jo. *Images of Ourselves: Women with Disabilities Talking*. London: Routledge and Kegan Paul, 1981.

Canadian Disability Rights Council and DisAbled Women's Network. *Four Discussion Papers on New Reproductive Technologies*. Winnipeg: CDRC and DAWN, 1990.

Carillo, Ann Cupolo, Katherine Corbett and Victoria Lewis. *No More Stares*. Berkeley, Ca.: Disability Rights Education and Defense Fund Inc., 1982.

Danforth, Pat, "Women with Disabilities." In *The Healthsharing Book: Resources for Canadian Women*, pp. 180-81. Edited by Kathleen McDonnell and Mariana Valverde. Toronto: The Women's Press, 1985.

DAWN Canada. *National Organizing Meeting of the DisAbled Women's Network, DAWN, Report, March 26-29, 1987, Winnipeg, Canada.* Vancouver: DAWN Canada, 1987.

D'Aubin, April, ed. *Breaking the Silence.* Winnipeg: Coalition of Provincial Organizations of the Handicapped, 1988.

D'Aubin, April. *Disabled Women's Issues: A COPOH Discussion Paper.* Winnipeg: Coalition of Provincial Organizations of the Handicapped, 1986.

D'Aubin, April, ed. *The Proceedings of COPOH's Workshop on Disabled Women's Issues.* Winnipeg: Coalition of Provincial Organizations of the Handicapped, 1987.

Deegan, Mary Jo and Nancy A. Brooks, eds. *Women and Disability, the Double Handicap.* New Jersey: Transaction Books, Rutgers University, 1985.

Degener, Theresia, *et. al. Geschlecht: behindert—Besonderes Merkmal: Frau. Ein Buch von behinderten Frauen.* (Sex: Disabled—Significant Feature: Female. A Book by Disabled Women). Munich: AG SPAK M68, 1985.

"Do 'crazy ladies' get raped?" *Phoenix Rising: The Outspoken Voice of Psychiatric Inmates* 1 (Winter 1981):15.

Doucette, Joanne, "Disabled women and poverty: double oppression," *Just Cause: A journal of law and people with disabilities* 5 (Fall 1987):13-15.

Doucette, Joanne, "Redefining Difference: Disabled Lesbians Resist," In *Lesbians in Canada,* Sharon Dale Stone, ed. Toronto: Between the Lines, 1990.

Doucette, Joanne. *Violent Acts Against Disabled Women.* Toronto: DisAbled Women's Network—Toronto, 1986.

Driedger, Diane, ed. *Aim At the Sky: Report of the Disabled Peoples' International North American and Caribbean Region, Disabled Women in Development Seminar, Roseau, Dominica, July 18-22, 1988.* Kingston, Jamaica: DPI North American and Caribbean Regional Secretariat, 1989.

Driedger, Diane. *The Last Civil Rights Movement: Disabled Peoples' International*. London and New York: C. Hurst & Co. and St. Martin's Press, 1989.

Driedger, Diane, "We Draw Strength From Each Other: Caribbean Disabled Women," In *Breaking the Silence*, pp. 104-109. Edited by April D'Aubin. Winnipeg: Coalition of Provincial Organizations of the Handicapped, 1988.

Driedger, Diane and April D'Aubin, "Disabled Women: International Profiles," *Caliper* XLI (March 1986):16-19.

Driedger, Diane and April D'Aubin, "Discarding the Shroud of Silence: An International Perspective on Violence, Women and Disability," *Canadian Woman Studies* 12 (Fall 1991): 81-83.

Driedger, Diane and April D'Aubin, "Literacy for Whom? Women with Disabilities Marginalized," *Women's Education des femmes* 8 (Winter 1991): 6-10.

Dueck, Susan Gray, "Stepping Stones to the Land of the Living," *Women's Education des femmes* 9 (Spring 1992): 13-15.

Duffy, Yvonne. ...*All Things Are Possible*. Ann Arbor, Michigan: A.J. Garvin and Associates, 1981.

Ellinger, Nina, "Forum 1985 in Retrospect," *Disabled Women's International Newsletter* 1 (June 1986): 10.

Feika, Irene, "The Big 'S' Word," *Conquest, Quarterly Magazine of Disabled Peoples' International North American and Caribbean Region* 1 (Jan. 1989): 16.

Fine, Michelle and Adrienne Asch, "Disabled Women: Sexism Without the Pedestal," *Journal of Sociology and Social Welfare* VIII (July 1981): 233-48.

Fine, Michelle and Adrienne Asch, eds. *Women with Disabilities: Essays in Disability, Culture and Politics*. Philadelphia: Temple University Press, 1988.

Gajerski-Cauley, Anne, ed. *Women, Development and Disability*. 2nd. ed. Winnipeg: Coalition of Provincial Organizations of the Handicapped, 1989.

Giraudel, Nathalie, " 'We Can Make It Work': Marriage and Blindness," *Conquest* 1 (Jan. 1989): 17.

Hannaford, Susan. *Living Outside Inside: A Disabled Woman's Experience. Towards a Social and Political Perspective*. Berkeley, Calif.: Canterbury Press, 1985.

Mairs, Nancy. *Plaintext: Deciphering a Woman's Life*. New York: Harper & Row, Pub., 1987.

Martin, Susan and the women of DAWN, "Disabled women and sex: 'We have successes and failures,'" *Kinesis* (Oct. 1986): 18, 19, 26.

Masuda, Shirley with Jillian Ridington. *Meeting Our Needs: Access Manual for Transition Houses*. DisAbled Women's Network, Canada, 1990.

McPherson, Cathy, "Vulnerable Victims of Assault," *Archetype* (1987): 16-18.

Morgan, Robin and Gloria Steinem, "The International Crime of Genital Mutilation," In Gloria Steinem, *Outrageous Acts and Everyday Rebellions*, pp. 292-300. New York: Holt, Reinhart, Winston, 1983.

Morris, Jenny, ed. *Able Lives: Women's experience of paralysis*. London: The Women's Press, Ltd., 1989

Owen, Mary Jane, "What's So Important About the Wrapping Paper on Our Souls?" *Rehabilitation Gazette* 27 (1986): 10-11.

Resources for Feminist Research, Toronto, Women and Disability Issue, 14 (1985).

Ridington, Jillian. *Beating the "Odds": Violence and Women with Disabilities, Position Paper 2*. Vancouver: DisAbled Women's Network Canada, 1989.

Ridington, Jillian. *Different Therefore Unequal: Employment and Women with Disabilities, Position Paper 4.* Vancouver: DisAbled Women's Network Canada, 1989.

Ridington, Jillian. *The Only Parent in the Neighborhood: Mothering and Women with Disabilities, Position Paper 3.* Vancouver: DisAbled Women's Network Canada, 1989.

Ridington, Jillian. *Who Do We Think We Are: Self-Image and Women with Disabilities, Position Paper 1.* Vancouver: DisAbled Women's Network Canada, 1989.

Rousso, Harilyn, with Susan Gushee and Mary Severance. *Disabled, Female, and Proud! Stories of Ten Women with Disabilities.* Boston: Exceptional Parent Press, 1988.

Sank, Cindy and Ellen Lafleche, "Special Sisters: Health Issues for Mentally Retarded Women," *off our backs* (May 1981):26-27.

Sawyer, Alison, "Women's bodies, men's decisions," *Phoenix Rising: The Outspoken Voice of Psychiatric Inmates* 1 (Winter 1981): 15-18.

Saxton, Marsha and Florence Howe, eds. *With Wings: An Anthology of Literature By and About Women with Disabilities.* New York: The Women's Press at City University of New York, 1987.

Schaefer, Nicola. *Does She Know She's There?* Toronto: Fitzhenry and Whiteside, 1978.

Stone, Sharon D. and Joanne Doucette, "Organizing the Marginalized: The DisAbled Women's Network," in *Social Movements/Social Change.* Frank Cunningham et al., eds. Toronto: Between the Lines, 1988.

Stuart, Meryn and Glynis Ellerington, "Unequal Access: Disabled Women's Exclusion from the Mainstream Women's Movement," *Women and Environments* 12 (Spring 1990): 16-19.

Tate, Denise and Nancy Hanlan Weston, "Women with Disabilities: An International Perspective," *Rehabilitation Literature* 43 (July/August 1982): 222-27.

United Nations, "Seminar on Disabled Women: Draft Report," Vienna, 20-24, August 1990.

Wheeler, Kelly and Gem Wirszilas, eds. *Visions of Flight: A journey of positive thought by and about women with disabilities.* Surrey, B.C.: By the Authors, 1991.

Winkelaar, Elizabeth, "Pregnancy and Spinal Cord Injury," *Rehabilitation Gazette* 27 (1986): 12-14.

Women with Disabilities Feminist Collective. *Women and Disability: An Issue.* Melbourne, Australia: Women with Disabilities Feminist Collective, 1987.

Zhang Li, "Pursuits," *Rehabilitation Gazette* 27 (1986):2-3.

CONTRIBUTORS

— ROSALLIE B. BUKUMUNHE, of Uganda, worked in a cooperative bank. She was involved in the Uganda Disabled Women's Association and has advocated for the rights and self-reliance of disabled women.

— TRUDY CLUTTERBAK, of Australia, is a feminist cartoonist and tram conductor.

— THERESIA DEGENER, of Germany, is freelance writer for German feminist and disability magazines. She is the co-author of several books on disability. She studied law in Frankfurt, Germany and Berkeley, USA. She is presently working on her PhD. where she is writing about the legal aspects of personal assistance services for disabled people.

— JIM DOHERTY, of the United States, is blind and is a freelance writer. He has a BA in journalism and he worked for the US federal government for 20 years as a writer/editor. He is interested in causes that promote opportunity and equality for people who are considered by society to be out of the mainstream.

— DIANE DRIEDGER, of Winnipeg, Canada, has been a nondisabled ally of the disabled people's movement for rights locally, nationally, regionally and internationally for the past twelve years. This includes work with the international and regional offices of Disabled Peoples' International in Winnipeg and Kingston, Jamaica respectively. She has also been involved in the independent living movement of disabled persons. She has a Master's degree in history, and her book, *The Last Civil Rights Movement: Disabled Peoples' International*, was published in 1989. She currently works with the Coalition of Provincial Organizations of the Handicapped (COPOH) as International Development Officer.

— NTIENSE BEN EDEMIKPONG was born in Ede Obuk-Eket in Akwa Ibom State of Nigeria on 11th November 1948, and was educated at the University of Ibadan, Nigeria. She obtained a Diploma in Religious Studies in 1977 and graduated from the Ecumenical Institute of Seminary Studies, Norwalk, California, USA, with a Bachelor of Theology in 1980. She has been a strong advocate of women's rights and joined the Women's Centre Eket, Nigeria, as a Patron in 1982. She has since then been Director of Research and author of articles of the Women's Centre.

— VENTURA EMMA : "I was born in Italy on 20th of April 1948 in a small town in the Marche region called San Severino M. I have always lived here and in 1964 I received my diploma in a secretarial school. In 1972, my book of poems was published. In 1974, I received a first place for my writing in a narrative competition and the following year this was translated into Greek and published in a Greek Anthology. In 1985, I received a first place in a narrative festival competition in Rome for handicapped people. In 1986, I received another first place in a similar festival competition in Milan."

— EUNICE FIORITO, of the United States, has been blind for the last 35 or 40 years. She currently works as an administrator in the US Department of Education, in Washington D.C.. She has a Master's degree in psychiatric social work from Colombia University. She started the first office for handicapped persons in New York City. Eunice was also the first president of the American Coalition of Citizens with Disabilities.

— BONITA JANZEN FRIESEN, of Canada: "As a child ('missionary kid') I spent some years in India. I attended Bible College, and then studied anthropology at university. From 1985 to 1988, I spent three years in Bangladesh under the Mennonite Central Committee administering a program for rural landless cooperatives. My perspective of disabled women in Bangladesh is limited to the interviews I conducted and my observations while working among rural women there. I am a wife, a mother and I am currently working with Hope International Development Agency as a program coordinator for their agraforestry program. I am based in Bangalore, India."

— EILEEN GIRON, of El Salvador in Central America, is working as the General Manager of a cooperative association of disabled persons called ACOGIPRI. She is on the board of directors of the Salvadoran Institute of Rehabilitation. Eileen was the Regional Development Officer for Central America for Disabled Peoples' International, 1985-88.

— SUSAN GRAY, of Winnipeg, Canada, is in a doctoral program in History at The University of Manitoba. She has worked as a Program Director for the Humanities and Professional Studies Area of The University of Manitoba's Continuing Education Division. Susan has also worked with the Society for Manitobans with Disabilities, with the Independent Living Resource Centre in Winnipeg, and as an English instructor at a local college. She has an interest in writing, especially in the short story. She also has a Master's degree in history.

— LESLEY HALL is a socialist feminist and disability rights activist from Melbourne, Australia. She has written many articles and reports on the rights of disabled people.

— JOYCE JOSEPH, of Trinidad and Tobago, in the Caribbean, runs a dressmaking business. She is active in Disabled Peoples' International Trinidad and Tobago, the self-help organization of disabled persons. She is also very active in church work.

— GERDA KLOSKE, of Germany, is blind and has been involved for nearly thirty years in volunteer work for the blind. She is a member of the German Federation of the Blind and a member of the World Blind Union's Committee on the Status of Blind Women. Her hobbies are: needlework, art history and archeology.

— ZHANG LI, of the People's Republic of China,: "My Afterthought, February 29, 1988. It was a great pleasure to write an article for this anthology. I wrote my article, "Battling With Adversity" by holding a pen in my mouth. I have overcome the difficulties caused by my disability with a strong will, learning to write in bed while holding the pen in my teeth. I devote my article as a present to this anthology and to friends—especially friends with disabilities."

— MARIA CRISTINA MATHIASON, of Austria, was born in Santiago de Chile in 1943. She is a graduate of Santiago College. In 1972, she was given the Shigemura Award for International Understanding by the Foundation for International Understanding Through Students in Seattle, Washington, USA. Since 1987, she has been living in Vienna, Austria where she is the representative of Disabled Peoples' International to the United Nations Office at Vienna. She is married and has two grown children.

— MIKIKO MISONO, Japan: "My birth was not wished for by mother. I was abused by her, raped by a teacher, and I have disabilities. But for all these social and physical tragedies, I have never degraded my dignity. I have chased happiness. Currently I am a student at Sophia University in Tokyo."

— YUKIKO OKA NAKANISHI of Japan: "From the Asia/Pacific Regional Office of the Disabled Peoples' International, which I had served since its founding, I worked at the United Nations Economic and Social Commission for Asia and the Pacific (ESCAP), 1986-1989. The project I worked on assisted national disability prevention and rehabilitation programs which are aimed at developing community-based rehabilitation in Bhutan, Bangladesh, Lao PDR, Maldives, Nepal and Vietnam. I have been president of the Asia Disability Institute since 1990."

— CATHERINE O'NEILL of Canada: "I have been a graphic artist, illustrator and mother for seven years now. I believe that we all have a responsibility for the future and should use whatever medium we can to bring about social and political change. I aim to comment, to provoke or to celebrate through my work."

— JULIANA ABENA OWUSU is the National Financial Secretary of the Ghana Society of the Physically Disabled, and a social worker with the Department of Social Welfare, in Kumasi, Ghana, West Africa.

— ELIZABETH SEMKIW, of Canada: "I did not know I was a political activist until someone referred to me as one. Who, me? If that is what you become when you are angered by unnecessary hardships and injustices for disadvantaged persons, such as children and people with disabilities, and try to convince those in power to change situations for the better, then that is what I am. Animals, music, nature and other less stressful pursuits fill the rest of my time."

— DR. FATIMA SHAH, of Pakistan, was, until recently the chairperson of the Women's Affairs Committee of Disabled Peoples' International (DPI). She was a member of the DPI World Council. She worked as an obstetrician-gynecologist and pioneer social worker in Pakistan, before losing her sight in 1955. In 1960 she founded the Pakistan Association of the Blind, a self-help organization. She was also active in founding of the Disabled Peoples Federation of Pakistan in 1982. She was a member of Parliament in Pakistan, 1980-84, where she represented the cause of women in general and people with disabilities in particular. She has won numerous awards from Pakistan and other countries, including the M.B.E. from Her Majesty the Queen in Britain, in 1962, for social services rendered to her country, and a Testimonial from the United Nations in 1987, in recognition of her support for the UN World Program of Action Concerning Disabled Persons.

— JUDITH A. SNOW, of Canada, works for Frontier College. She graduated from York University in 1976 with a Master of Arts in Clinical and Counselling Psychology. She worked with the Canadian Association for Community Living for over nine years. She is also the chairperson of the Attendant Care Action Coalition, a group of more than sixty organizations and individuals who are lobbying for individualized funding for attendant care serices.

— T. CHRISTINA F. STUMMER, of Brazil, is deeply involved in transportation issues through the disabled persons' group in Sao Paulo. She will be returning to school in the near future in either law or a social work graduate program. She is currently working as a free-lance translator in English, Spanish, French and Italian. Writing an autobiography is also in her plans.

— AMBER COVERDALE SUMRALL, of the United States, is co-editor of *Touching Fire: Erotic Writing by Women; Women of the 14th Moon: Writings on Menopause; Sexual Harrassment: Women Speak Out* and *Catholic Girls*. She is editor of *Lovers: Stories by Women* and *Write to the Heart: Wit and Wisdom by Women Writers*. She lives in Santa Cruz, California.

— ROSEMARY WEBB, of Northern Ireland, United Kingdom, was born in Belfast, Northern Ireland and educated in England. She is widowed, with three married daughters, has nine grandchildren and lately, great-grandchildren. She was at one time a prison visitor, member of the Juvenile Court Panel, a member of Remand School Boards and a member of the Police Authority for Northern Ireland for 10 years. She became disabled in 1970 and she was awarded the M.B.E. in New Year's Honor List and received it from Her Majesty the Queen at Buckingham Palace in 1983.

— JAYNE C. M. WHYTE, of Canada, has been a consumer of mental health services since 1966, and active in the Canadian Mental Health Association since 1975. She is a freelance writer who continues to work in advocacy and volunteer with community organizations. She lives in Fort Qu'Appelle, Saskatchewan.

— GEM WIRSZILAS, of Canada: "I was born April 24, 1936 in Sumas, Washington, where the nearest hospital was located. I have lived within 100 miles of Vancouver all my life. I taught school for three years, but retired to live on a small hobby farm after my marriage 33 years ago. We have four adult children and are a close-knit family. I enjoy the needle arts, horticulture, reading, playing the accordian and singing off-key. Until recently, supporting a political party and voting in elections was all that political activism meant to me."

— ZANA, of the United States: "I'm forty-five, Jewish, disabled with arthritis, scoliosis, allergies. I live on land with other lesbians. My writing and art has appeared in many lesbian and feminist publications in the USA. I have published a book of poems and drawings, entitled, *herb womon*."

INDEX

ACROSS BORDERS

WOMEN WITH DISABILITIES WORKING TOGETHER

EDITED BY DIANE DRIEDGER, IRENE FEIKA AND EILEEN GIRÓN BATRES

This book portrays the multifaceted work by women with disabilities from the developed and developing world. Through literacy and economic development projects, and community organizing, women with disabilities collaborate to improve their standard of living and create new opportunities. Personal stories combine with political activism in topical accounts from around the world. *Across Borders* illustrates how women can learn from each other and grow together — across many kinds of borders.

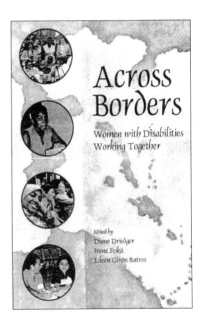

176 pp
ISBN 0-921881-38-X
$16.95/$14.95 U.S

Gynergy books titles are available at quality bookstores. Individual, prepaid orders may be sent to: **gynergy books**, P.O. Box 2023, Charlottetown, Prince Edward Island, Canada C1A 7N7. Please add postage and handling ($3 for the first book and $1 for each additional book) to your order. Canadian residents add 7% GST to total amount. GST registration number R104383120. Prices are subject to change without notice.